Bakery Design

Bakery Design

images
Publishing

Contents

Preface

01

By Athanasios Tzokas

Athanasios Tzokas was born in Kalamata, Greece, and grew up under the influence of his father, who ran TZOKAS architects. After graduating from the d'Annunzio University of Pescara in Italy, Athanasios returned to Greece, and took over the management of his father's architectural office before taking charge of many distinctive and successful projects ranging from interiors and building design to large residential complexes, as well as graphic and logo design.

Contemporary dining spaces

Due to the progressive development of cultures, the consumption of food—which is essential—became a social affair. Dining spaces, thus, were transformed into social areas where visitors were able to converse with each other as they consumed food. Dining spaces were also shaped by the ritual of the preparation itself, which varies across cultures and the time of the day.

In the digital age, this ritual has further evolved—in fact, radically. With the advent of social media, personal food and eating experiences have gone online for the world to see. People now not only consume the food, they also consume the images that are being transmitted via social media. These uploaded photographs on social media have, for many, become an integral piece of the eating ritual.

These changes have brought about the need to transform modern food preparation and eating areas to meet the new needs and requirements of visitors in the digital age (Figure 01, 02).

The bakery phenomenon

The history of bakeries spans back to the Roman Empire and, as such, the typology of bakery design has changed a lot over hundreds of years. Today, with the digital influence, we are in a new age of bakery design.

From antiquity, bread has been one of the basic foods for much of the world. Over time, the preparation and consumption of bread became integrated into culture itself. The wheat-farming population, who incorporated the reaping and breadmaking into their culture, considered themselves civilized, as opposed to tribal cultures who primarily consumed meat.

With the development of a more sophisticated gastronomic culture within populations over the centuries, bread products began to acquire a greater value and wider variety.

01 Photography: João Morgado
02 Photography: Zach Hone
03-04 Photography: Ströck

02

03

04

The sale of bread within bakeries became part of a larger product line including sweet and savory items, coffee, and other beverages. Simultaneously, the varieties of breads themselves also developed and expanded to adapt to consumer tastes, needs, and aesthetic desires.

The neighborhood bakery has changed into not only supplying bread as a staple, but also a large variety of sweets, delicacies and quick breakfast and lunch solutions for those on the go, thus acquiring a hybrid character combining the typologies of the traditional bakery, the grocery, and the café in a hospitable space.

In many cases, bakeries have even developed into very alluring spaces, offering an attraction within themselves. This is apparent in all the following case studies. In some cases, the typologies of bakery or dessert shop co-exist with other typologies, such as bar or restaurant.

The Ströck Feierabend in Austria (Figure 03, 04), for instance, is an innovative concept that functions as a fully operational bakery during the day and as a restaurant and wine bar at night.

05

06

Also, the TiensTiens in China (Figure 05, 06) is a French dessert shop, the roof of which and surrounding buildings are used as a bar at night.

The real situation

Due to economic downturn, many enterprises were confronted with bankruptcy and despair about their futures, forcing a reduction in growth of dining places. As such, Europe created new economic programs to encourage people to establish new enterprises and strengthen the employment via business dexterity. Thus, cafeterias and bakeries began to pop up like mushrooms, without solid business plans or specific target groups, even in regions with a limited purchasing public. The growing percentage of these ventures did not have favorable endings either. Through this market slump, the survivors realized that the only solution was to create quality products in combination with beautifully designed spaces.

Design is the solution

Bread—and its more recent derivative products—is a familiar staple food for consumers, with a history spanning back hundreds of years. As such, one question to be considered by operators in contemporary bakery design is: should the design of the space maintain a familiar aesthetic to be instantly recognizable as a bakery to modern consumers?

Contemporary requirements are not only dictated by the changes in the product range and the needs of consumers, but also by modern socio-economic conditions, all of which need to be taken into account in redesigning bakeries. The goods for sale and the rituals of their preparation and consumption have considerably evolved over the years. As a result, the planning in bakery design also needs redefinition.

Thus, architects and designers are tasked with creating new places of production and, often, consumption of bakery products. Taking into consideration this hybrid character of contemporary bakeries, their design needs are multifaceted. The modern

07

08

bakery should incorporate the requirements of the production process, the consumer consumption space within the bakery, and the products' promotion, which includes creating a unified identity through the logo and design.

The approach in planning, therefore, needs to first address the following questions:

- Which product characterizes the bakery and which ones are supplementary?
- What is the target group and what kind of customer turnaround is anticipated for both counter sales and those dining in?
- Are the products produced at the time of the order or are they prepackaged?
- Is the manufacturing process important to the customers?
- Will the customers purchase at the counter or will staff offer table service?
- Is there a need for a home-delivery service?
- What kind of staffing will be available throughout the day?

The production area

Historically, the baker's production area was the *only* space in a bakery. With modern requirements, the baking space had acquired a purely functional role and is not necessarily visible to the customer, like a manufacturing lab. Thus, the large ovens that were traditionally found in the dominant position within the store have been moved into the back, freeing space for the promotion of more products.

However, in some cases the production process of the bakery products is visible to the consumer in a more distinctive way. In Cheese Tart Shop 'BAKE' in Ho Chi Minh City in Vietnam, designed by 07BEACH and Joe Chikamori (Figure 07), the production area is visible from the stair-shape entrance. The staffs work on tart-display tables while the customers can observe them as they enter the bakery.

The Pain Paulin Bakery in France by Ciguë (Figure 08), is also an example. The lab opens onto the street and the bakery's production processes are visible to passersby.

05-06 Photography: Chen Hao
07 Photography: Hiroyuki Oki
08 Photography: Maris Mezulis

09 Photography: fragments.cat
10 Photography: Yiannis Fais
11 Photography: Aytekin Demircioğlu
12 Photography: I IN
13-14 Photography: João Morgado

The product promotion area

In new-generation bakeries, promotion is just as important as production, as their image is also being consumed by the clientele. The variety of products and the need for properly displaying them to the consumer—combined with increasing competition—has transformed the bakery spaces into "jewelry shops," exhibiting the bagels, muffins, and quiches like diamond rings under glass. This change brought with it new elements to consider in the furnishings of the space, such as showcases, also with a reconfiguration of the bakery layout itself.

The product ranges are displayed neatly in glass showcases to be as attractive as possible to customers. Design creates the solution to how the products are presented and promoted, hence, the materials, colors, and lighting are important design tools in highlighting the quality of the goods.

In Ferrer Xocolata in Spain by Arnau estudi d'arquitectura (Figure 09) and in Savoidakis Bakery & Patisserie in Greece by Manousos Leontarakis & Associates (Figure 10), the products are displayed in glass showcases. On the other hand, in Grandma Bakery Café— Nişantaşı in Turkey by Zemberek Design (Figure 11), and in Pinocchio in Japan by I IN (Figure 12), the showcases are open, aspiring to give the customer a close and unhindered connection with the product, as much as possible.

The consumption area

With the changes mentioned above, in addition to the increase of available commodities, consumers inevitably take longer to get to know the products being sold. This need was met by creating more space (and in some cases tables and chairs) for the consumption of the bakery items, which prolonged the customer's stay in the shop.

This new addition to the bakery typology, the consumption area, is perhaps the most important difference to traditional bakeries of the past. The consumption area may vary in scale and atmosphere depending on the importance of the consumption process for the business, as well as the desired time of the customer's stay in the store. In some cases, it occupies a small area in the form of a counter, minimizing the consumption time, while in other bakeries, it is in the form of tables and chairs, resembling those of cafeterias or restaurants. In the latter case, the residence time is lengthened and the products offered are usually more than just snacks or pastries; rather, small prepared meals. In such cases, the contemporary bakery has expanded into a type of fast food outlet or even a restaurant by changing the boundaries between different dining places.

This design is apparent in many of the following case studies. One of them is the Bakery by Paulo Merlini (Figure 13, 14) where the consumption area was the

13

14

15 Photography: Imagen Subliminal, Miguel de Guzmán
16-17 Photography: Peter Dixie for LOTAN Architectural Photography
18 Photography: Toshiyuki Yano
19 Photography: The Strangely Good, OWMF Architecture
20 Photography: Hey! Cheese Photography

main design tool. They created three different environments so that customers would be able to select a space more befitting their mood and feel more comfortable.

Creating the bakery's identity through design

The identity of the business should also be defined as unique and competitive from the design and architecture of the store itself. The need to project, maintain, and create a unique corporate identity must be anticipated and achieved—and also within budgetary constraints—as this is the key to its success. Identity can be defined by a unique architectural element, which has emerged from the design and differentiates the space from the already known conditions.

Another approach in successful bakery design is to create a space that makes visitors feel at home. A more intimate environment, using natural materials such as wood or marble, can entice customers into the venue and promote comfort.

In Patisserie III in Spain (Figure 15), ideo arquitectura created an artistic installation: 12,000-plus wooden magenta sticks hung from the ceiling. The installation with its strong character competes with the consistency of the 150-year-old framed wall and creates a unique bakery's identity.

Location and visibility in the city

The location, scale, and the role of the bakery in the city are also important elements to be considered in the design. Increasing downtown rent prices in many cities have led young entrepreneurs to choose smaller venues or venues located in neighborhoods further from the center.

As far as small-scale spaces are concerned, the design needs to satisfy the above requirements in a limited space. Necessities such as productive workspace, product visibility, and visitor hospitality should be satisfied in a comfortable and inspiring

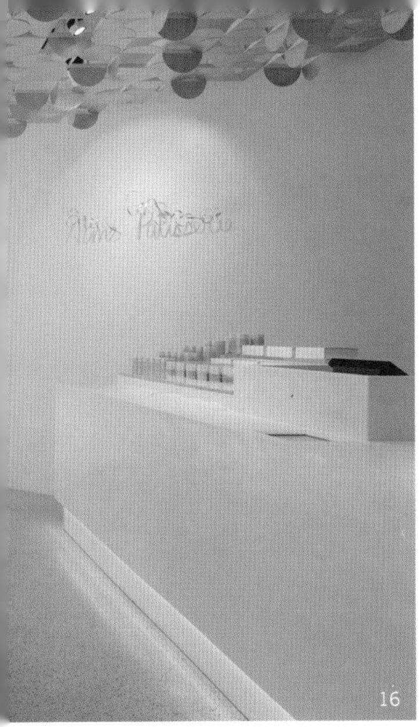

16

17

18

environment with unique, flexible solutions. In a small shop, proprietors should be offering quality over quantity.

There are many instances where one can find successfully designed small spaces, between 215 and 645 square feet (20 and 60 square meters). Some examples include The White Gift Box (Figure 16), Pantry's Best—the Tree (Figure 17), Tôt le Matin Boulangerie (Figure 18), and Suzette (Figure 19).

19

The Home Bakery in China by Fulhouse (Figure 20) is also an example of a small-scale project that uses an interesting design to counter its small size. The overall area is 237 square feet (22 square meters), and the interior is only about 13 feet (4 meters) high, so the professional kitchen is tucked into a glass box behind the kitchen island.

The strategic location of the store in the city is certainly a predominant criterion for the success of a business, but an eye-catching shop is also able to create attraction in any neighborhood, which increases opportunity for clientele.

20

The store should be visible to consumers even when it is not situated in the center of the city. The "wow effect" is the goal of provoking passersby to notice the shop. Spending excessive amounts to implement this is not necessarily the solution; rather, it requires a unique approach to obtain the desired effect, whether it is spatial-architectural or color-decorative. In summary, it takes boldness.

In conclusion

Food has been a necessity, of course, since the dawn of time, and quickly also evolved into a means of socialization. Bread has long been a staple food in the Western world and changes that have occurred over time to both the production of bread and bakery foods and the consumption processes of people have had a heavy influence on the evolution of the design of bakeries.

With the dawn of the digital age, further factors have come to the fore that must be taken into account in the design process. The wide variety of available products, the need to create a unique identity, the prevalence of new food patterns, and—more recently—the influence of social media on the predominance of image, versus taste, have created the new model for dining spaces, leaving the traditional typology unable to satisfy modern requirements. As such, modern bakeries must be designed according to contemporary needs.

In addition, changes in production processes and availability of goods have led to increasing numbers of items for sale in bakeries. Bread is no longer the predominant product, it coexists beside a variety of sweets, pastries, and beverages. With such variety has evolved a need for promoting and displaying the offerings to consumer, which has become more imperative to success.

The need for more display and promotion space, coupled with changes in production, has, predominately, led to the removal of the oven from the main bakery area. In most cases, the consumer no longer receives the product at the time of its preparation, but instead in its final, well-presented form beneath a glass display case, like a "jewelry shop" of baked goods, far removed from traditional neighborhood bakeries where the mixing, kneading, and baking of dough by the baker were a natural sight in the bread-buying process.

As such, the need for successful design is now more imperative than ever in this new hybrid typology, which needs to wed the bakery, grocery store, coffee shop, and even restaurant into one place to capture a significant market. The new bakery aspires to provide consumers with a variety of well-presented goods, to be as attractive as possible, and to maintain a welcoming environment, often in a small city space.

A growing number of bakeries in both inner-city and suburban locations has called for the need to stand out in the crowd to capture a market share, which has led to the need to create a unique and competitive business identity. While proprietors need to supply quality goods and a welcoming environment in order to achieve this, architecture and design should also play a significant part in making the business visible to the public, drawing in customers, and enticing them to stay within the shop for as long as possible to increase potential sales.

With the use of natural materials—which create an inviting familiarity to the public—and the correct design choices, architects and designers can create a suitable environment to service both the business and consumers, while simultaneously responding to contemporary needs. Each design choice and well-considered solution to requirements affect overall customer appeal and, ultimately, the success of the business.

ne artigianale

Case Studies

Addictive chocolate world

- **Project name**
  Ferrer Xocolata
- **Location**
  Olot, Spain
- **Site area**
  2583 square feet
  (240 square meters)
- **Completion**
  2015
- **Interior design**
  Arnau estudi d'arquitectura (Arnau Vergés Tejero)
- **Photography**
  fragments.cat (Marc Torra)

Building a dream is not easy, but that was the commission. While many people have this goal, this commission was like no other—it was the reform of a building as a workshop for chocolate cakes, pastries, pies, and cookies.

The designers had to renovate an old building in order to create a space entirely devoted to chocolate. That was the sweet dream of Jordi, the chocolate maker. The designers had to do it with emotion, with metaphors, with a sense of humor. They sought the whimsy of Easter cakes and chocolate chickens!

In order to make it happen, the designers needed to enter the client's dream. They observed where the chocolate is produced, onsite in the basement, which used to be an old storehouse for salted cod. The product is then molded, set, and sold in the shop. The façade of the shop, as such, was created from chocolate tile molds used in the chocolate-making process. Behind it, there is a vertical space that was born out of the effort to connect the five levels of the building. To achieve this, they relied on the staircase and its visual omnipresence as

well as on the different passing gaps that link vertically the three lower levels.

Everything was specially designed in this project: from the section of the building to the chairs in the tasting area and the chocolate tiles. It was a global and absorbing project, which turned out to be very addictive for the designers, who even got to taste it!

la moda

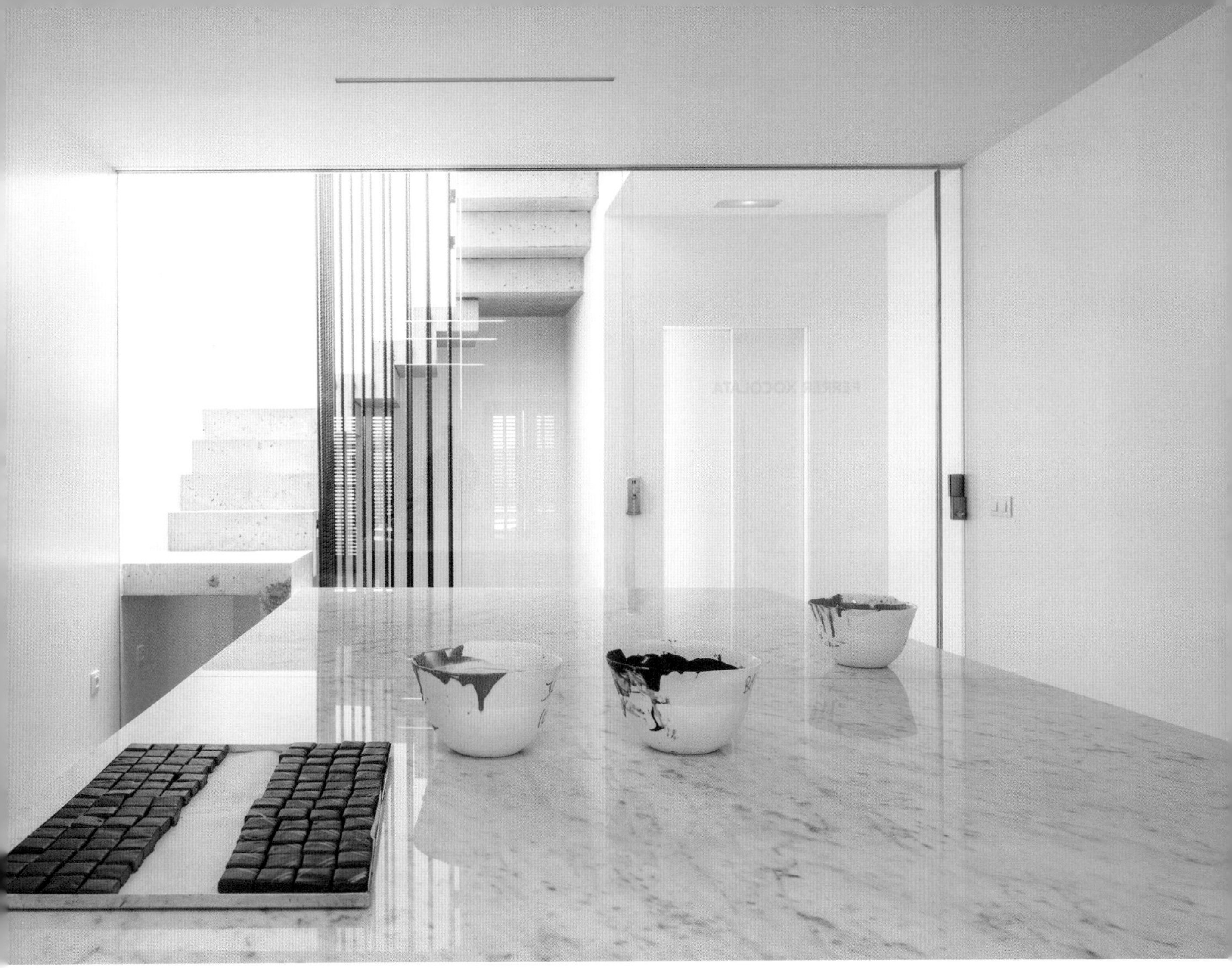

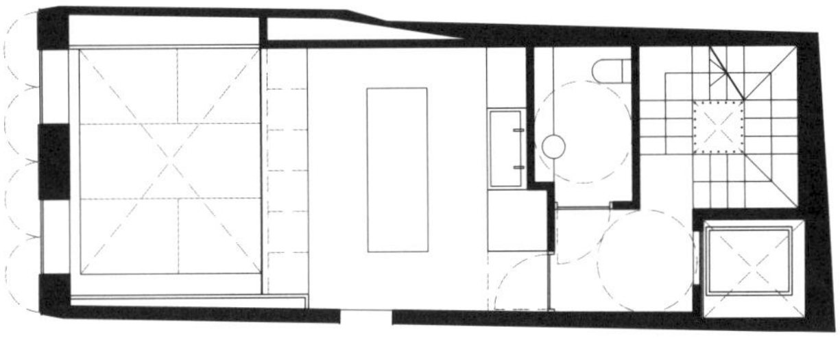

Second-floor plan

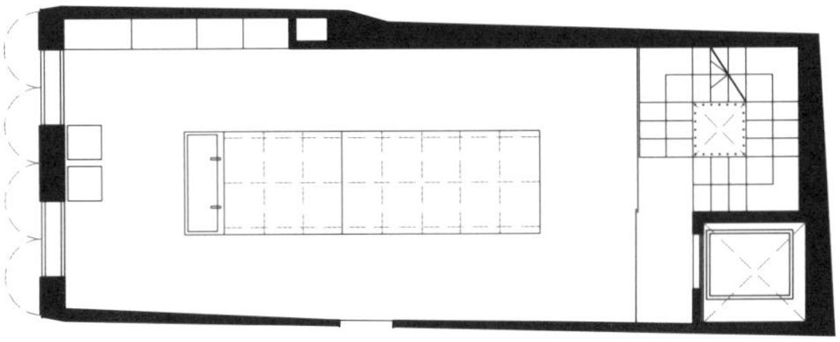

Third-floor plan

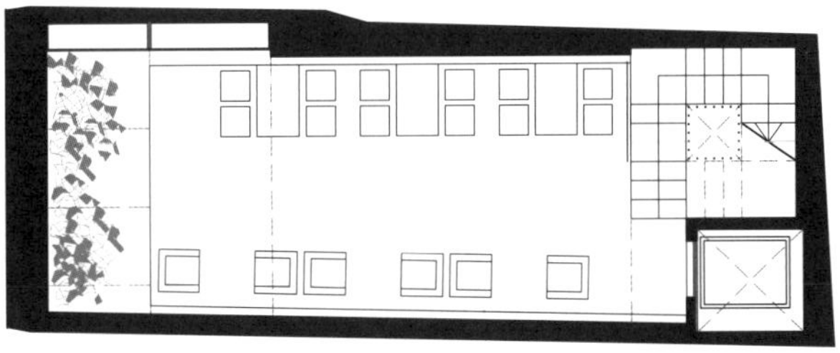

Basement plan

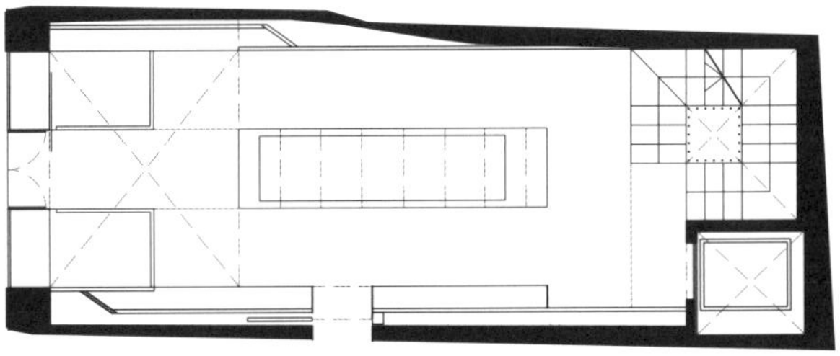

First-floor plan

Mai no trobaràs una excusa
per no menjar xocolata

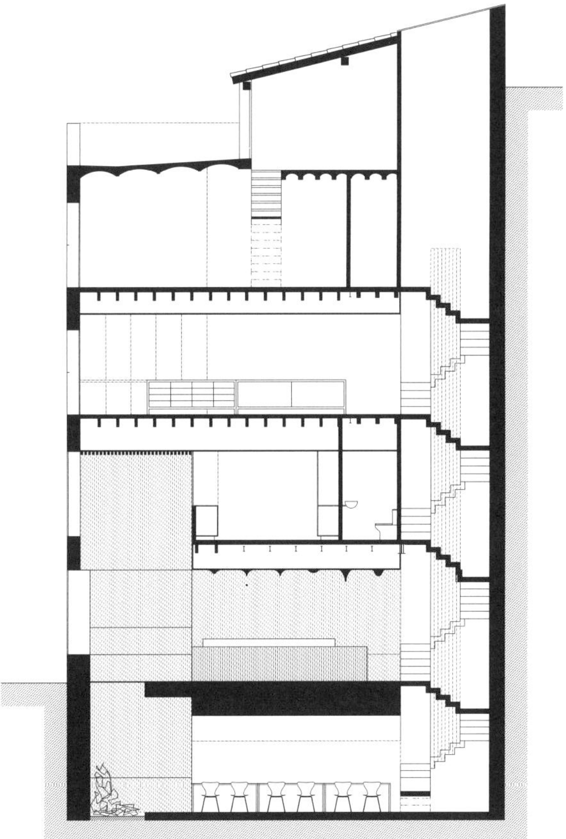

Section

Revival of the traditional Greek grocery

- **Project name**
  Lalaggi Bakery
- **Location**
  Kalamata, Greece
- **Site area**
  732 square feet
  (68 square meters)
- **Completion**
  2016
- **Interior design**
  TZOKAS architects
- **Photography**
  AthanasiosTzokas, Alex Papageorgiou

The central idea behind the design of this business was inspired by the revival of the traditional Greek grocery store and the contrasting minimalism of the modern world. The gap was bridged by the combination of traditional furniture and simple parallelogram shapes that blend with one another. Thus, the antiquated wood, the handmade furniture, and the natural materials came in contrast with the sharp surfaces made of lacquered wood and glass with the radiant blue walls that complete the whole setting.

The blending did not stop at the materials, but was also transferred to the relationship between employee and customer, since there isn't a physical barrier between them. There is just a notional line from the geometrical motif created by handmade cement tiling.

The multiple drawers, apart from their classical storage, also act as a showcase for small products. The main goal with the pre-packaged products is to encourage customers to serve themselves.

Correspondingly, beneath the worktable is hidden a second surface, which doubles the functional surface space or, upon demand, restricts the space of the coffee machine, creating a small bar.

Great importance was given to the lighting, in order to allow the owner to have the ability to highlight by targeting the illumination at certain products that he would like to promote.

The central table is the main attraction and is the only one placed diagonally into the room, which allows for easy movement around it while also capturing the clients' attention.

Due to the fact that the store is 31.5 inches (80 centimeters) below the level of the external road, a small elevation was created in part of the façade where, in combination with the sliding glass, the high table becomes functional for both internal and external seating.

The name of the shop, "Lalaggi," comes from the crispy strips of dough, coiled in random spirals, reminiscent of Plumen lamps, which are exhibited in the shop window.

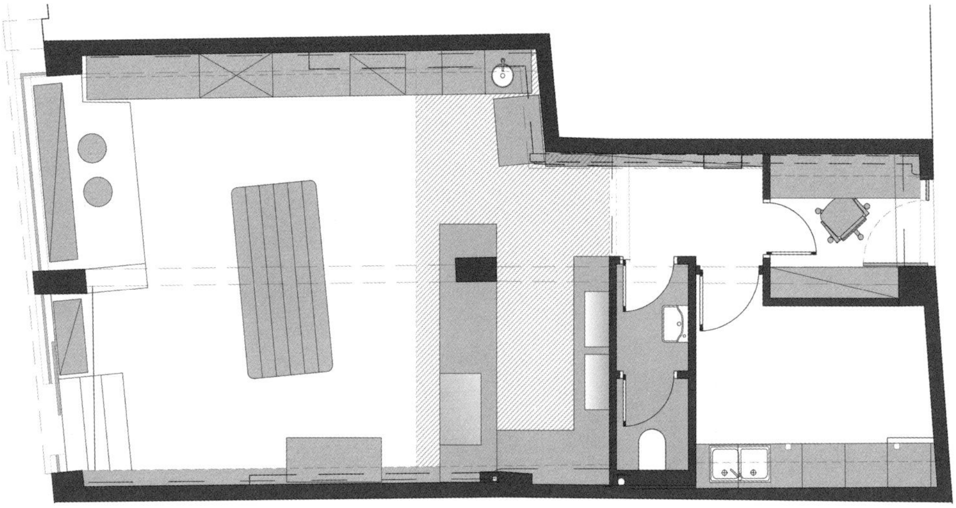

Plan

Rendering

Dreamy French minimalism

- **Project name**
  Nanan
- **Location**
  Wroclaw, Poland
- **Site area**
  1033 square feet
  (96 square meters)
- **Completion**
  2016
- **Interior design**
  BUCK.STUDIO
- **Photography**
  PION

Nanan is a modern patisserie for those with a sweet tooth. As such, sweets play the leading role in the signature design of this modern patisserie. The deliberately minimalist interior provides a subtle setting for the main attraction: the finely decorated, sophisticated cakes and éclairs, which are made with meticulous care.

The specialty of this patisserie, the éclair, inspired the interior design and the visual identity of Nanan. The cake's oval shape is echoed in the central island counter with a display that operates almost like a glass cabinet in a jeweler's shop. Its positioning provides room for the flow of customers, who can choose and admire trays of tempting bijou sweets and small works of confectionary art. It gives a feeling of being part of a sweet feast rather than in the queue in front of a pastry shop counter.

The éclairs also inspired the bespoke design of lamps and other details of the interior, such as mirrors, door handles, coat hangers, and veneer perforation. An

éclair motif naturally lent itself to the patisserie's visual identification. Color and material choice for Nanan was, on the other hand, an embodiment of the second inspiration for the project—Marie Antoinette and the vision of how her parlor would look in modern times.

The aim was to create a representation of ambience that is feminine and carefree but in a modern form, using current means of expression. For this reason, pink was chosen as a statement color but it was used in a really synthetic way—as a minimalist omnipresent background.

So, the whole place was given the context, with velvet, pink walls with arched doorways. Combined with pink marble tops and delicate shining brass details, it builds a surreal ambience of a soft and dreamy landscape. It is a place where time seems to stop and customers can forget about the whole world.

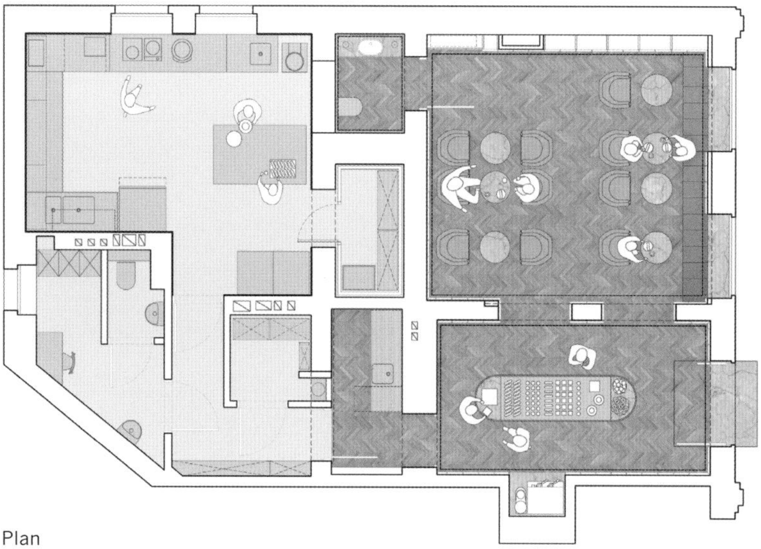

Plan

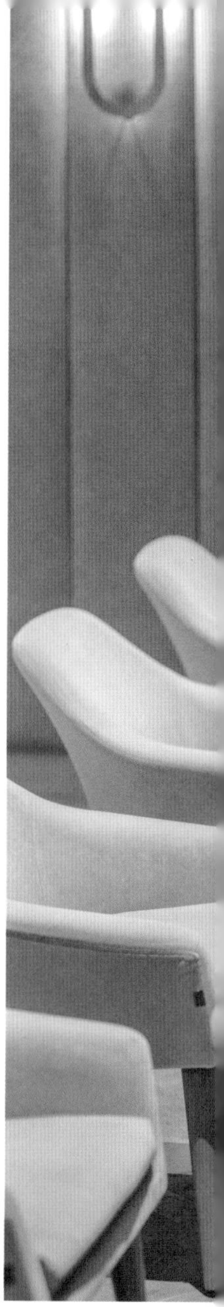

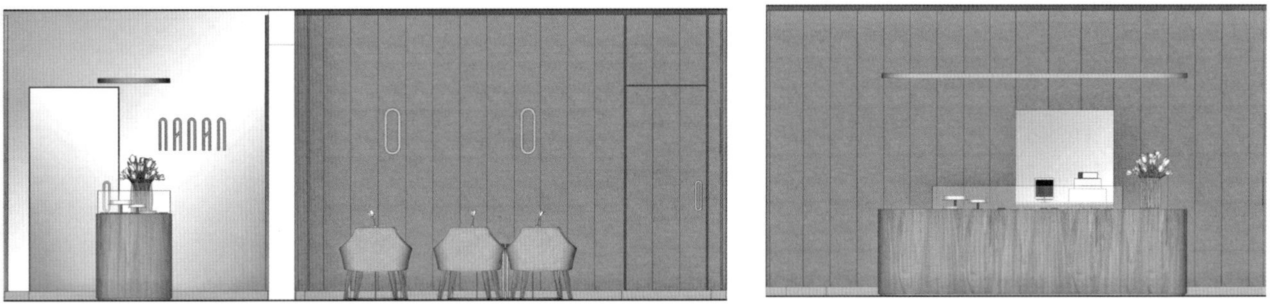

Section

Wooden magenta sticks hanging from the ceiling

- **Project name**
  Patisserie III
- **Location**
  Madrid, Spain
- **Site area**
  592 square feet
  (55 square meters)
- **Completion**
  2015
- **Interior design**
  ideo arquitectura
- **Photography**
  Imagen Subliminal, Miguel de Guzmán

The project was to design the client's third bakery in Madrid, which makes bread and cakes. As the client believed that every bakery should be unique and different to their others, the only specific design request was the use of their cooperate color, magenta.

The site was on a ground floor of an interesting old building in the historic center of the town of Alcala de Henares. As soon as the designers demolished the internal walls and cleaned up the façade, they realized that the existing brick walls were filled with a history that spoke for itself, giving the space a huge personality.

In order to achieve a contemporary design, which was the initial objective, the designers had to find an element with a strong character that would compete with the consistency of the 150-year-old framed walls without eclipsing them. Therefore, they created an artistic installation: 12,000-plus wooden magenta sticks hung from the ceiling. This installation attracts

much attention! The color magenta is not very common in interior design and, in this case, the designers used this color very well to deliver the full visual impact. At the same time, the thousands of wooden magenta sticks coexist with the pink of the bakery's floor. The exposed walls create a sense of simplicity.

In addition, the architect and designer from ideo arquitectura, Virginia del Barco, designed the lighting as a part of the furniture within the chairs, the stools, the shelves, the bar top, the whiteboards, the light boxes in the façades, and so forth. One can appreciate the different details of the claddings, as well as the high-quality microcement pavements, which give the space a refined elegance. Customers can not only enjoy the delicious food in the space, but can also feel the exquisite life.

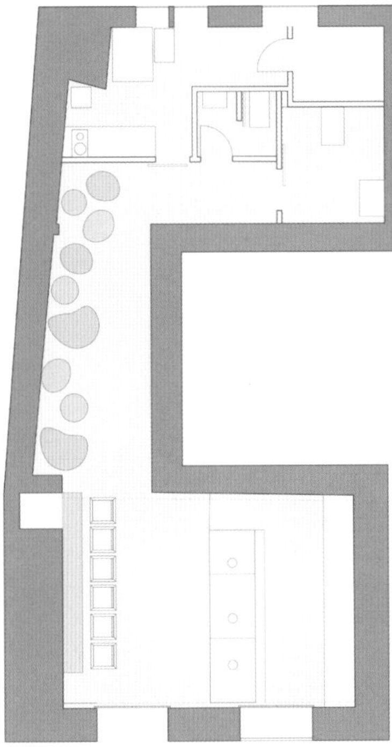

Plan

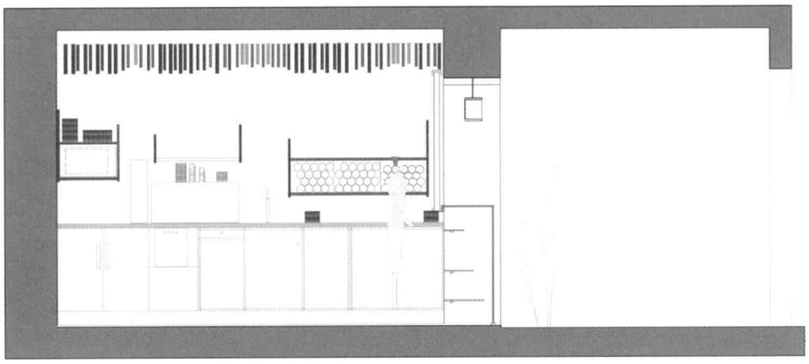

Section

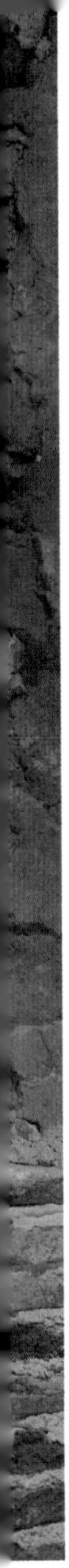

Intertwinement of ceiling and wicker baskets

- **Project name**
  Au Pain Doré
- **Location**
  Côte-Des-Neiges, Montreal, Canada
- **Site area**
  1500 square feet
  (139 square meters)
- **Completion**
  2014
- **Interior design**
  naturehumaine
- **Photography**
  Adrien Williams

This project invites people to re-evaluate the idea of a contemporary bakery. The main challenge was to preserve the warm and welcoming interior atmosphere of this type of business without trying to imitate the aesthetic codes of the ancestral bakery adorned with wicker baskets and varnished wooden furniture. In sum, it was necessary to preserve this "cozy" feeling while developing an attractive new concept.

The façade deceives the eye, as upon entering the designers discovered that the bakery had significant depth. The different spaces were structured from the operational diagram of the space. The barista—an important part of this bakery—is central and positioned in the foreground to be identifiable from the outside.

The originality of the project came from the fact that the ceiling is a structuring element of architectural planning. An architectural and ornamental element, the ceiling is freed from all the display constraints related to the operation of

the business that apply to the walls. The ceiling takes advantage of the long typology of the place by deploying its structure in all its length. The spatial concept of the project is inspired by wicker baskets in which the bread was transported and preserved, like intertwining reeds. Transcribed on an architectural scale and reinterpreted, this idea was transformed into a random arrangement of poplar slats that rush with a breath of dynamism in the bakery to bring warmth to the space.

By turning vertically on the wall, the device becomes an indispensable functional support that integrates different elements. Modular slats turn into shelves for breads and pastries or in seating and countertops. Black steel brackets make it possible to fix these elements as well as the display supports necessary for the operation of the trade.

Finally, the enveloping shape of the device scrambles to abolish the perception of the ceiling height of the interior, causing an illusory distortion of space. The result is a shop where the warm atmosphere invites you to indulge. It feels like being wrapped in a comforting, intimate, and resolutely contemporary space.

SOUPES DU JOUR
MINI SANDWICHS
SANDWICHS
SALADES MAISON
QUICHES
PIZZAS

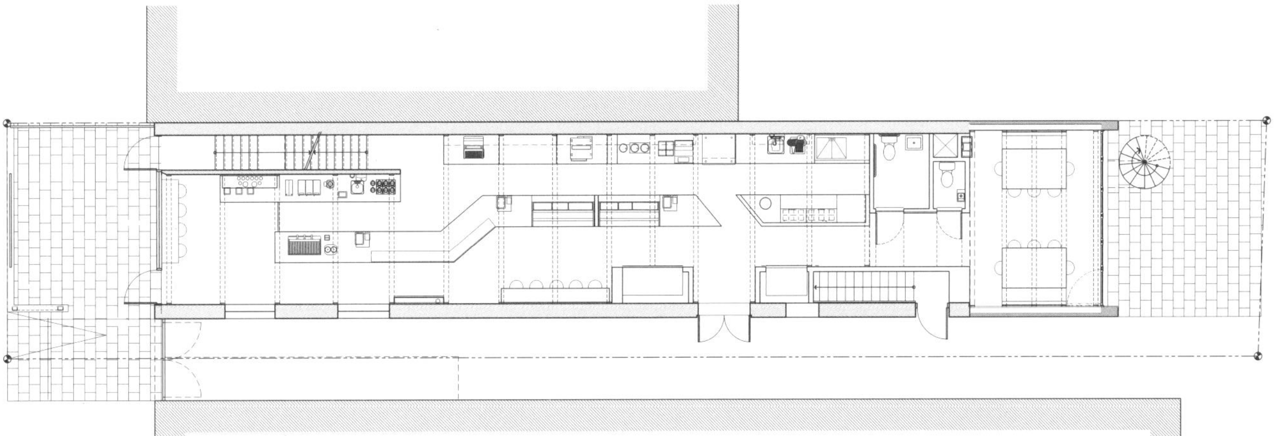

Plan

Cozy atmosphere created by vintage woods

- **Project name**
  Baffi Alimentari
- **Location**
  Bergamo, Italy
- **Site area**
  1292 square feet
  (120 square meters)
- **Completion**
  2016
- **Interior design**
  Margstudio
- **Photography**
  Sara Magni

This project called for a redesign of Baffi Alimentari, situated in a shop with a history of over 50 years. The restructuring focused attention on the history of this family and the materials that identified their working lives.

In order to stand out from the tangerine-pink wall of the old building, the designer chose white as the color of the background of the logo plaque on the façade. As a result, pedestrians can see the internal space at a glance when passing by. The use of large glass doors also allows for excellent visibility from the street, enticing customers to stop.

The material chosen for the interior was primarily wood, creating a warm feeling. The rustic texture juxtaposes a vintage quality against a modern, linear atmosphere to make the space both cozy and captivating. Bread, cakes, and all kinds of food are mainly displayed in paper bags or placed directly on the white shelves; glass was placed on top of wooden shelves to display the delicious selection.

At the central area of the shop, wooden food shelves were well-integrated with black baffle, making the entire space look simple and neat. Unlike many other bakeries, instead of displaying only a few food items, nearly all the food in the Baffi Alimentari is on display, creating a gastronomic atmosphere to entice visitors sitting and eating there.

In addition to various kinds of bread, cakes, pastry, snacks, and other baked good, Baffi Alimentari also sells jams, candies, chocolate desserts, and some materials for baking at home. The whole space seems to be a baking paradise!

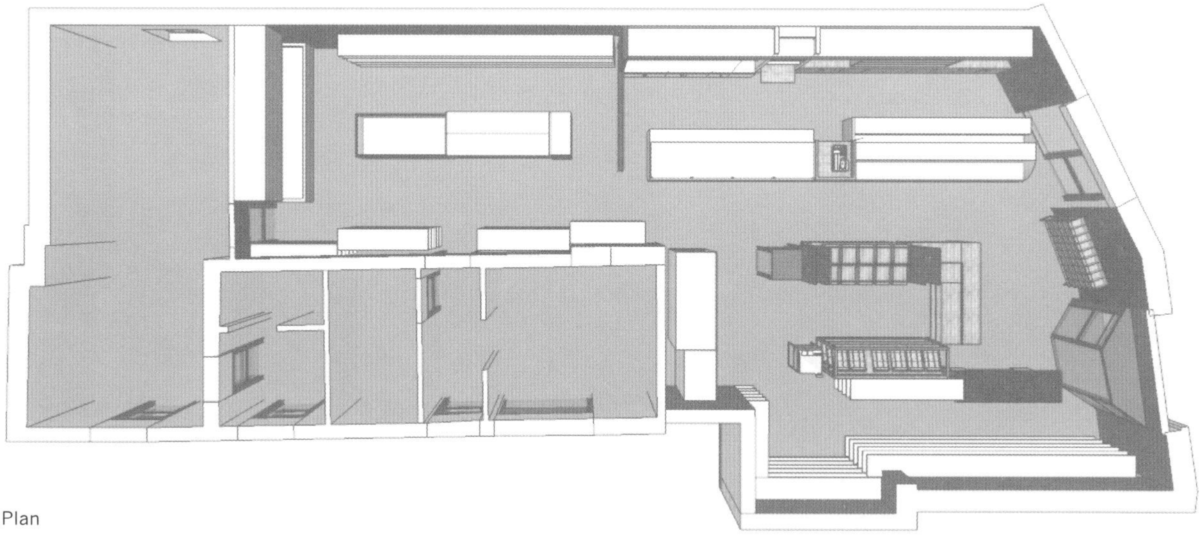

Plan

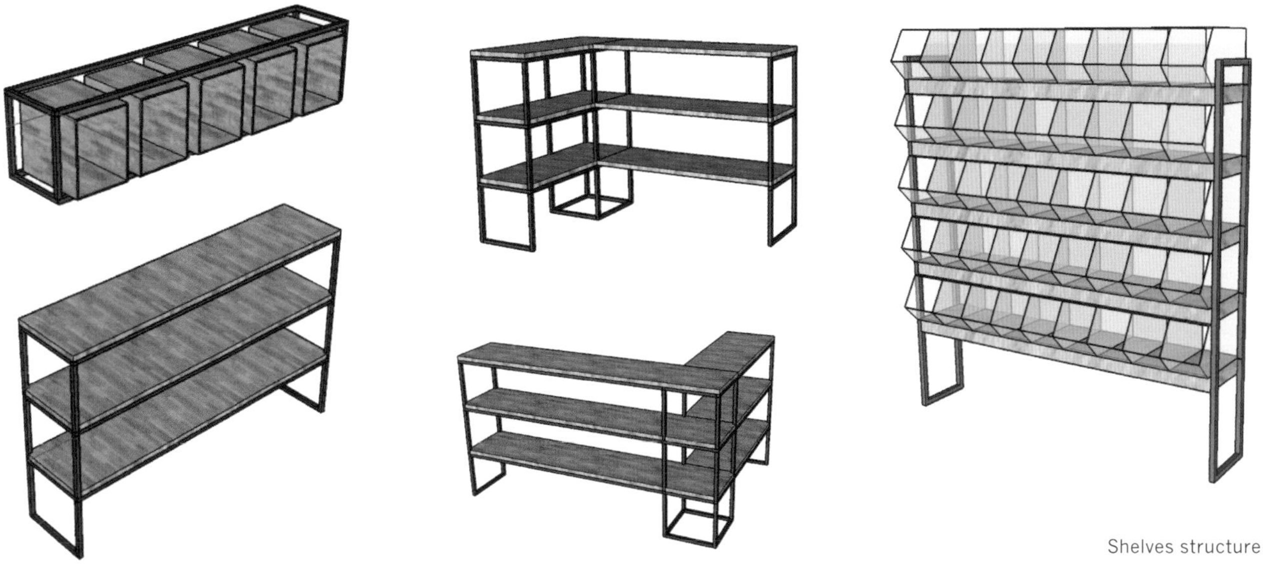

Shelves structure

The “melt” ceiling

- **Project name**
  Bakery by Paulo Merlini
- **Location**
  Gondomar, Porto, Portugal
- **Site area**
  4951 square feet
  (460 square meters)
- **Completion**
  2013
- **Interior design**
  Paulo Merlini arquitectura
- **Photography**
  João Morgado

Before undertaking this project, the designers visited and analyzed similar spaces to try to find errors that could be corrected. They found that a basic error being committed was that most of these services only had one type of space. This design approach ignored the variation of moods people feel during the day—whether they come in with alone, with friends, are looking for a place to read a book, or to socialize. So, to bridge this flaw, they created three different environments so that customers would be able to select a space more befitting their mood, rather than have to adapt to one atmosphere. This way, they provided a more emphatic place and consequently tripled the commercial potential.

But a customer isn’t a customer until they’re through the door. So, the question of enticing the customer inside the bakery needed to be addressed by the designers.

In a metropolitan lifestyle, everyday people deal with millions of inputs, like billboards, signs, other people, cars, and so forth. The way the brain deals with this excessive

information is to send most of it to the unconscious mind, releasing the conscious from the excessive information. As one moves through the city, the brain captures the information around and gathers all the similar inputs creating a mental “scenario” that, based on predictability, is perceived by the unconscious mind, releasing the conscious to all variable inputs that are being experienced outside that scenario. This is a survival system that was inherited from the savanna era, which ensured that if, for example, a predator moved between the trees, a person—without having to consciously capture every bit of information around—could perceive the movement and react to protect their own life.

Coupling this with the fact that 70 percent of those inputs are visual, and that humans, like many animals, are attracted to light, the designers knew that they had to create an input that could distinguish itself from the rest of the city scenario in such a way that it could activate the conscious perception, guaranteeing that people would notice and feel attracted to it. For that, they used light as the main attraction. They studied the approximation of the observer to the space and realized that the most visually relevant plan from the exterior was the ceiling and, so, they focused on that.

From studies, the designers also discovered that the use of direct light tends to heat up the space and create shadowed corners turning space into uninviting places and that, in an auditory approach, the excessive noise mainly resulting from the reverberating sound was not being properly solved. So, to solve these problems they knew they had to break the sound waves and refract the light. And so they did, by creating a second ceiling that results from the repetition of wooden stripes, they found a system that could solve the two problems in a row.

In their research they found studies that prove that the presence of color and forms that are like food actually make people hungrier. So to invoke that in customers they picked the 20 most-wanted products of the bakery and, based on a pattern of global identification, they found a middle tone and applied it on the walls. On the formal approach, they made the ceiling "melt" in some points to make it look like a cake topping or icing.

The designers also proposed a new logo to the client, and designed the space partially based on it. The wooden stripes descend through two of the walls creating an effect that dialogs directly with the consumer. When one moves through the space, some hidden forms start to appear on the walls. Those forms are an abstraction of the proposed logo. The intention is to unconsciously reinforce the image of the firm in one's mind.

They like to think of their interventions as positive manipulation of the human brain. As such, they focused on giving positive inputs to all the five senses (where possible) so that they can alter ones homeostatic level, and, as a result, make people feel happier.

Perspective

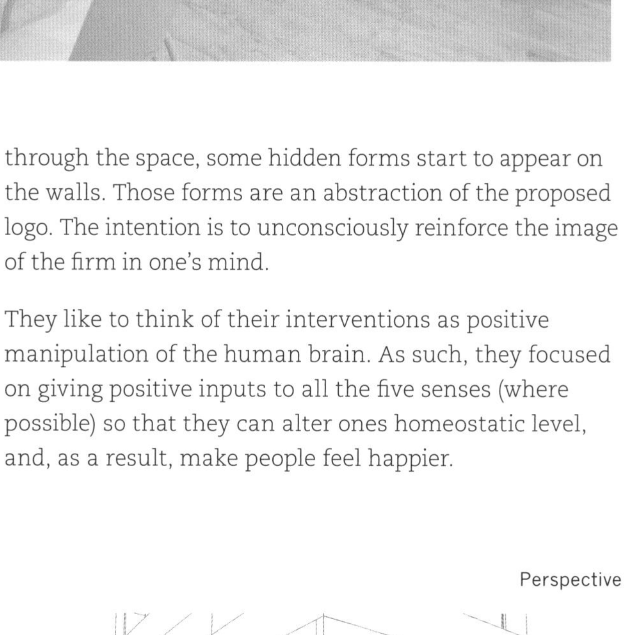

Sections

Plan

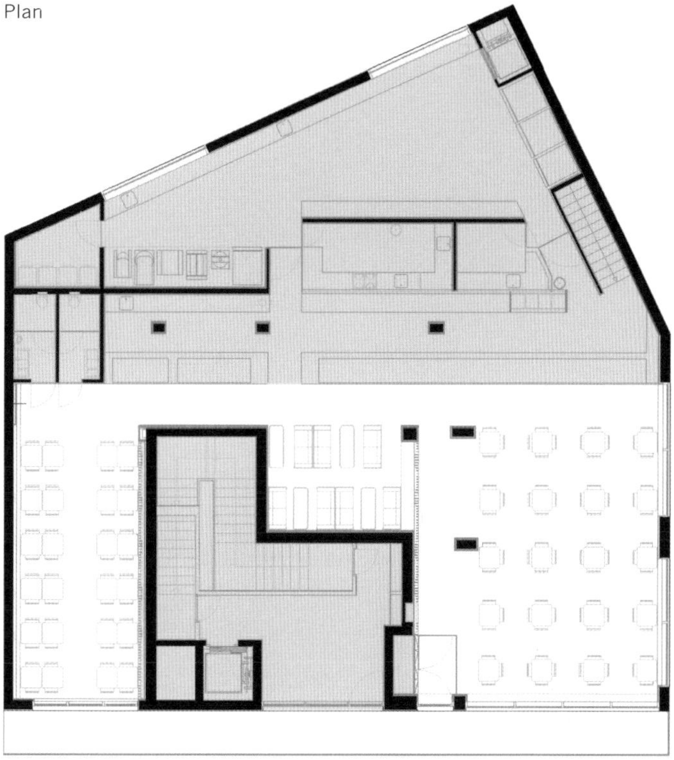

Art deco of burnt baking trays

- **Project name**
  Doppio Cafe Bistro
- **Location**
  Toruń, Poland
- **Site area**
  646 square feet
  (60 square meters)
- **Completion**
  2014
- **Interior design**
  mode:lina™
- **Photography**
  Marcin Ratajczak

Bartkowscy is a family bakery that was established in 1927. Today it has 18 stores in Torun, Poland. In 2014, in cooperation with mode:lina™, the owners created a new place with a unique character in Aleja Solidarnosci in Torun: Doppio Cafe Bistro.

The meeting with the centenarian history of the family's craftsmanship was a huge inspiration in designing the new interior. The aroma of fresh bread, huge ovens, and old worn-out baking sheets made it clear to the architects that the fusion of traditional and modern designs was the answer. Old burnt baking trays were found in a store during an inventory and used to build a decorative wall and lighting elements. They received a second life as wall décor and lamp shades. The traditional atmosphere is omnipresent thanks to oven-shaped furniture and natural wood mixed with small white enamel tiling. The counter and lighting were finished by meticulously selected wooden planks that link to traditional oven fuel. The final touch was the black-and-white mosaic floor that is

reminiscent of the old stores. Near the glass window, the designers set out the seating simply. These wooden seats echoed with the wooden counters, creating a sense of warmth in rustic simplicity.

mode:lina™ often choose unusual materials because they like to experiment. They go for materials that contain a kind of identity element, characteristic for a given project. Using the old baking trays, the designers created a unique effect. At the same time, the trays highlight the combination between retro and modern.

Designers always look for interesting inspirations in what their client tells them about themselves. These could sometimes be very simple elements, at times almost unnoticeable, yet it is their task to notice and turn them into something functional and aesthetic. They search for an idea that would become the main theme of the project. The element of surprise is important! This is another reason why the designers used the old burnt baking tray. The interior is not only functional and welcoming, but also memorable.

SZYNKA + INDYK
WEGE
WŁOSKA
KURCZAK
MEKSYK
Latte mała 7 zł duża 8 zł wielka 9 zł
Latte macchiato duża 8 zł
Mocha mała 8 zł duża 9 zł
Cappucino duża 7 zł
Frappe duża 8 zł wielka 10 zł
Smoothie duża 8 zł wielka 10 zł
Czarna mała 5 zł duża 6 zł wielka 7 zł
Biała mała 5 zł duża 6 zł wielka 7 zł
Gorąca czekolada mała 6 zł duża 8 zł
Herbata mała 4 zł duża 5 zł

DOPPIO

Sketch

Baking room in retro industrial design

- **Project name**
  Biga Bakery & Café
- **Location**
  Caesarea, Israel
- **Site area**
  1292 square feet
  (120 square meters)
- **Completion**
  2017
- **Interior design**
  Eti Dentes Interior Design
- **Photography**
  Yoav Peled

The Biga ("biga" is an Italian bread-baking technique) chain started out as a small bakery in a little town in the north of Israel and has become a well-known establishment with more than 20 stores around the country.

The brand values are quality ingredients, meticulous processes, and the bakers' love for their art, which result in a unique flavor. The designers conveyed the joy of baking and manual handling of the dough through an experiential visual language of illustrations taken from the world of baking and bread making. At the same time, it was important to preserve the values of simplicity and good taste and to convey the meticulousness of the bakers' work and great passion for pastries and baking.

Located in an industrial area at Caesarea, surrounded by factories and offices, this 1292-square-foot (120-square-meter) store has a very low ceiling, surrounded by glass panels. The challenge was to design a small café with a little bakery to supply the

local workers, especially at breakfast and lunch times. The materials used and the color palette was based on simplicity and a factory feeling: black and white with hints of fresh green and oak—colors reminiscent of breads and pastries.

All the walls at the serving areas were covered with simple white and green tiles. Along the longest wall in the store, a long brown leather sofa was located and the wall was covered with wood panels with brand graphic-design elements and custom made iron wall lamps to provide a cozy and intimal feeling. At the corner between the café counter with the seating area, the small shop counter with black iron and retro industrial glass included shelves with products to buy and take home.

Graphic black-and-white tiles were used at the floor and oak panels were used to cover the recessed ceiling above the bar where the air-conditioning and other systems were located. To complete the industrial vibe, black acoustic tiles was used. The space combines deli, pastry shop, and café and the clients can smell of the aroma of home-baked cookies and breads from the entrance.

B*
מאז 1999
ACQUA E FARINA
לחמי מחמצת
BISCOTTI
נאפה במקום
FRESH טרי
מאפים
BAGUETTE
בריוש
PASTERIES
CROISSANT
פוקצ'ות
B*
artisan bakery
BIGA
Boulangerie

Boulangerie
artisan bakery
artisan bakery
אפיה בעבודת יד
BIGA
BIGA

BiGA
מטבח · בייקרי · קפה
B*
artisan bakery
Boulangerie
aqua e farina
מחמצת באיטלקית

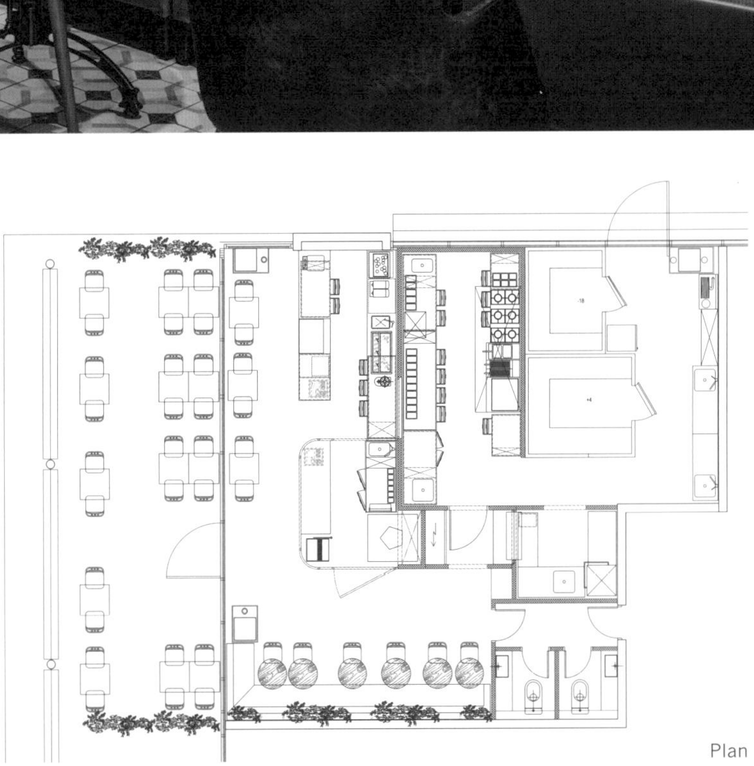

Plan

Pure artisanal space design

- **Project name**
  Bread & Hearth
- **Location**
  Singapore
- **Site area**
  1076 square feet
  (100 square meters)
- **Completion**
  2014
- **Interior design**
  Studio SKLIM
- **Photography**
  Béton Brut (Khoo Guo Jie)

Nestled in the heart of the former red-light quarters of Keong Saik Road, Singapore and among gentrified shop houses resides Bread & Hearth—an artisanal bakery.

Taking branding cues from the bakery's name, brick was chosen as the ubiquitous material to construct most of the spatial concepts. Bricks are predominantly used as architectural building blocks. In this instance, the material configures itself to form both exterior and interior, structural and non-structural elements in the form of frontage, counter tops, ventilation holes, furniture, partitions, and floor. The limits of the material are tested with both linear and double curvature geometries, construction joints and tiling patterns.

Programmatically, the functions of seating, display, service, kitchen, and back-of-house are distinctly lined up in a linear configuration due to the nature of the shop house. The spatial sequence upon entry is almost funnel-like and slowly opens up to a full-fledged brick wall with a geometrically

challenging coffee station. Each block of brick counter houses a distinct function (bread, viennoiseries, cashier/control center, and coffee station) and is staggered to permit more standing space and interaction with the baked products. Bricks are strategically removed from the dividing kitchen wall to permit both smells and visual sightlines to the inner workings of the kitchen.

To permit a greater flexibility in the arrangement of bread displays, pegboard was used to line an entire wall. Custom canvas shelves were also designed as miniature hammocks to display the bread in linen bags, creating a softer and playful contrast to the hard-edged brick modules. In reference to the character of the shop house, the underside of the wooden staircase was intentionally expressed and reinterpreted as the menu board for the bakery.

The craft in artisanal bakery was taken as a reference to the details in the shop, which included a variety of brick tiling methods and also reflected in the choice of custom furniture. The free-standing tables and stools take reference from the traditional craft of constructing furniture with mortise and tendon joints, further adding to the atmosphere of craft and detail synonymous with the craft of baking.

Diagram

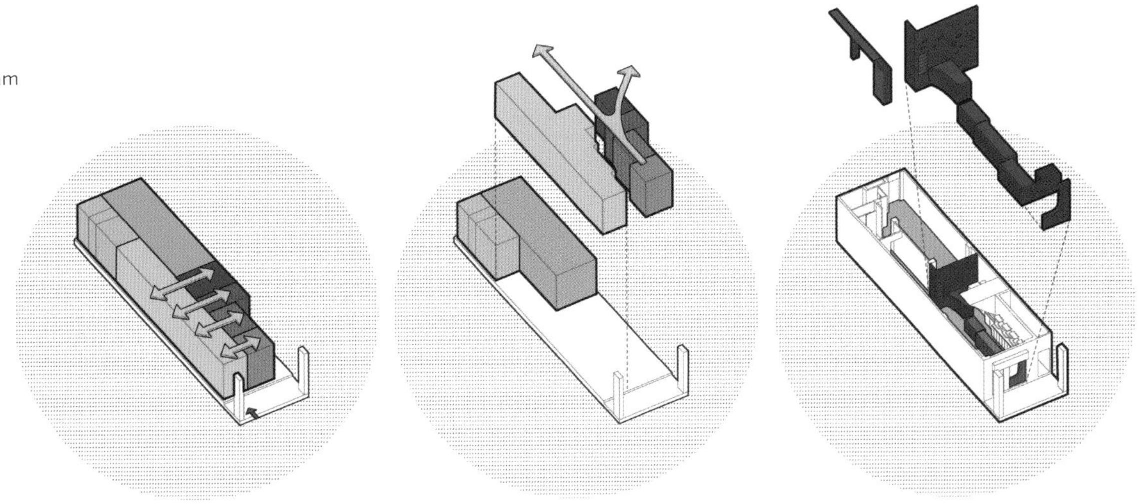

Plan

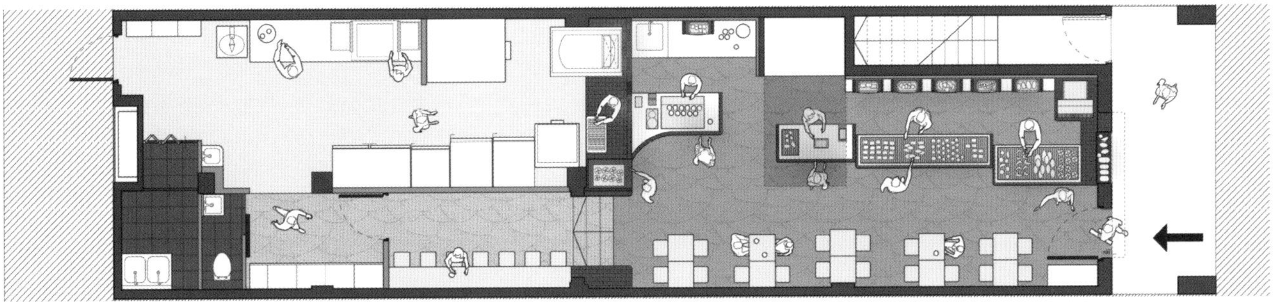

Pink space full of fun

- **Project name**
  Bribery Bakery
- **Location**
  Austin, United States
- **Site area**
  1780 square feet
  (165 square meters)
- **Completion**
  2016
- **Interior design**
  Design Hound
- **Photography**
  Ryan Farnau and Robert Lerma

Bribery Bakery, located at Austin, Texas, was completed by local company Design Hound. It was open to the public in 2016, with an energetic look to all visitors. People always ask why Jodi Elliott chose the name "Bribery" for the outpost selling her baked goods and cocktails—frankly, it was one of the first questions the designers asked her when she contacted them—it refers to baked goods as 'bribes' for good behavior.

This type of tongue-in-cheek play on what one normally associates with dark, back-alley deals became the starting point of the design for this bar and food destination in the Mueller neighborhood of Austin.

From that beginning idea of turning Bribery on its head and making it a fun and light-filled space that families would enjoy, Design Hound worked to add as much of Chef Elliott's larger-than-life personality into the space as possible. Exterior accents of powder-coated pink entry doors, a matching display case, and vinyl decals reminiscent of cake

decorations attract the attention of daytime passersby.

Inside the space, large swaths of flocked pink wallpaper line the perimeter, while the teal-and-white-faced bar area beckons customers to approach the display case, the marble bar top, and the liquor-lined shelves. Backed with mirrors and supported by brass-bar railing components, the shine on most of the surfaces is eye-catching and fun. Seating comes in the shape of black-and-white patterned stools, pink upholstered chairs, and vertical-tufted camel-colored banquettes with pink feet.

As night approaches and the sunlight begins to fade, the interior of the space, with its eye-catching pink neon sculpture running from the front of the soffit by the entry all the way to the display case, transforms into something very different. It is finally a slightly dim, but still fun, pink cocktail bar where "the ladies go and the men will follow" per Chef Elliott.

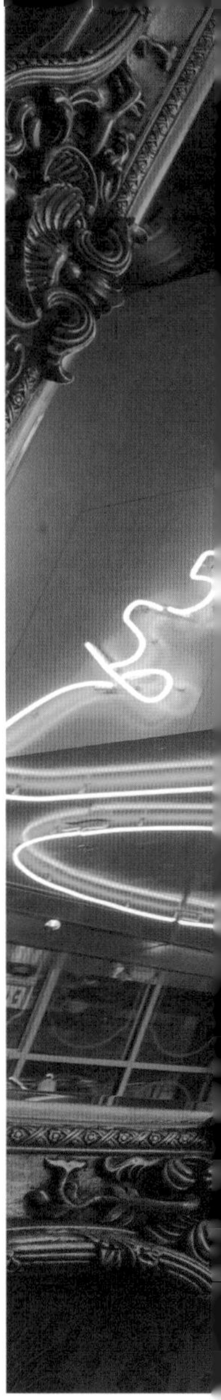

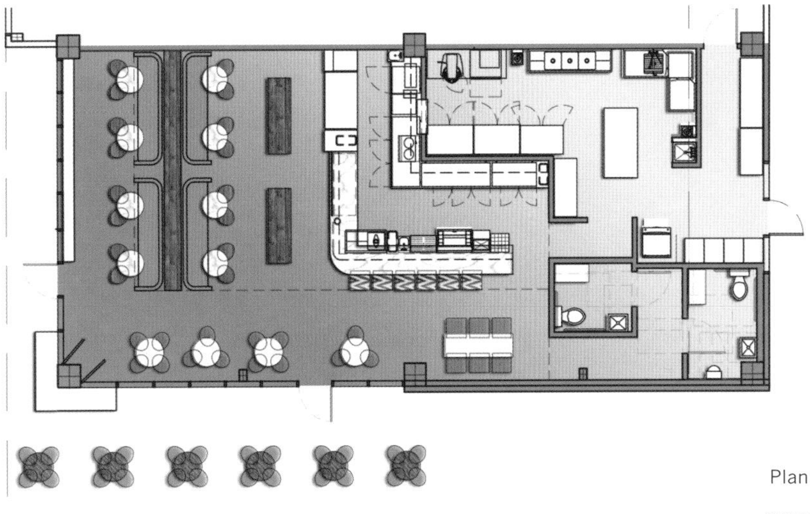

Plan

The warm freshness

- **Project name**
  Café Liebes Bisschen
- **Location**
  Hamburg, Germany
- **Site area**
  1507 square feet
  (140 square meters)
- **Completion**
  2016
- **Interior design**
  PARAT
- **Photography**
  Andreas Meichsner

PARAT was asked to design the interior for a new café run by pâtissiers Hamburger Tortenmanufaktur. Named Liebes Bisschen, the space combines references to the 1950s with a contemporary palette of colors and materials.

The layout has been restructured to create a generously proportioned front-of-shop hospitality space with a small salon and the bakery looking back out onto the interior courtyard. Seamless Terrazzo-style designer screed was used to maintain a unified color concept throughout the café.

On each side of the main room, upholstered benches were placed along the walls; the table groups towards the center of the space feature a range of colors and seating. Small potted plants on each table embellish the interior space and give people a fresh and pleasant feeling. In front of the rear wall, a long counter marks the end of the open room. Structured into two parts by wooden paneling on the one side and a signet on

the other, the counter also houses an inset glass display for cakes, tartes, and gateaux.

With its window into the bakery, the backroom offers a quiet space for customers and can also be used for bookings. Its table is tailored to fit around the free-standing column at the center of the room, while wall shelving and a chandelier made of teak make for a homely ambiance.

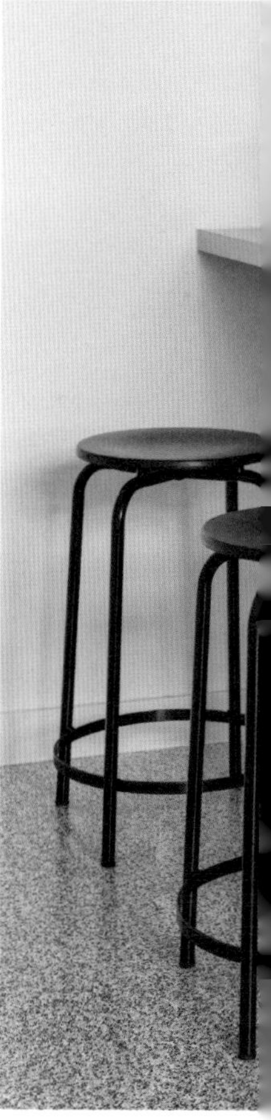

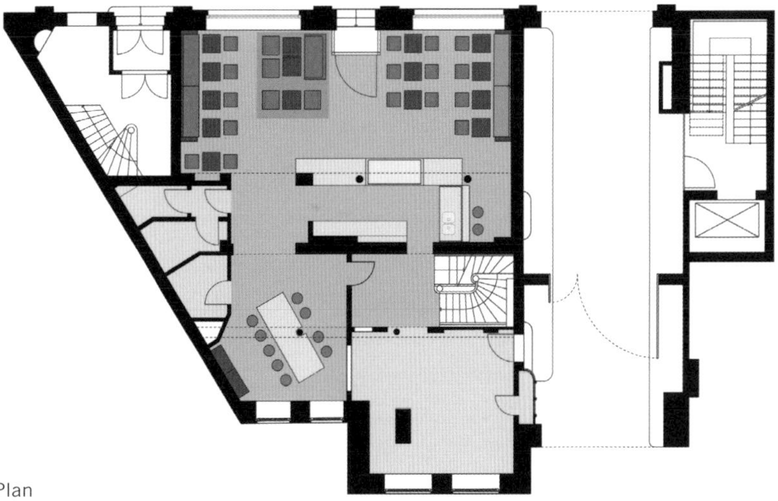

Plan

Attractive stair-shape entrance

- **Project name**
  Cheese Tart Shop 'BAKE' in Ho Chi Minh City
- **Location**
  Ho Chi Minh City, Vietnam
- **Site area**
  749 square feet (69.6 square meters)
- **Completion**
  2017
- **Interior design**
  07BEACH, Joe Chikamori
- **Photography**
  Hiroyuki Oki

Many bake stores are located in shopping centers and railway stations with customers queuing at the store front. To stand out from other bakeries, Cheese Tart Shop 'BAKE' chose to utilize the property configuration, which faces a street and has a double-height ceiling.

First, the stairs from the entrance to the cashier were designed to show passersby that customers were to queue in a vertical direction. They also made each tart-display table—where staff worked—a different height to follow the stairs and inside floor. The varying floor height was of concern to the client, who thought it could create a tripping-hazard for staff; however, a safe solution was reached by gently sloping the interior floor following the incline of the exterior staircase dimensions.

An essential requirement of the brief was to show the inside openly rather than constructing an optical border between the staff and customers. Therefore, it was decided that the tables would be

held with a point-fixing bolt attached to the glass to minimize obstruction. The client was, again, concerned that this approach wouldn't be stable enough. However, the designer felt it would offer a sense of newness to the ordinary taking a different approach, so after consulting the manufacturer, they decided to change the single leg into a double for extra support, and also check a handrail that was held with the point-fixing bolt to a glass. Finally the idea was approved, provisionally, with the strength to be confirmed with a mock-up.

In computer rendering, the designer applied different lightnesses on each surface to emphasize a shape of an object. He then took that approach by applying a lighter color of mortar on horizontal surfaces and darker on the vertical to emphasize the staircase's shape. Convinced it would be interesting, he tried it in an actual construction. Like emphasizing a face's features by shading it with makeup, he thought that the figure of the stairs could be surreptitiously emphasized by using different colors of mortar. Deciding on the right two colors, aiming at a natural appearance, was not easy. Many different lightness of mortar were compared and the conclusion was reached that two obviously different colors can still appear natural if side-by-side at 90 degrees, like stairs. A mock-up of the stairs was then painted with the two

selected colors under sunlight, with the final color being slightly adjusted.

A lighter color of mortar was also applied to the walls on the staff side and darker on the customer side, with more light being given to the staff area in order to highlight it like a stage. Over the duration of the project, drawings had to be repeatedly amended for the client to overcome concerns with strength and safety. Turning down an idea when concerned is easy; however, thanks to the fact that the clients valued design as a major advantage of the brand, the designers were able to have positive discussions and could realize the ideas rather than taking an easier, uninspired approach.

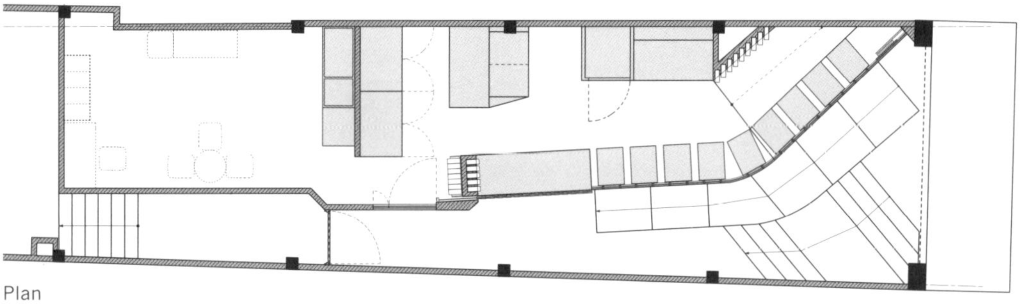

Plan

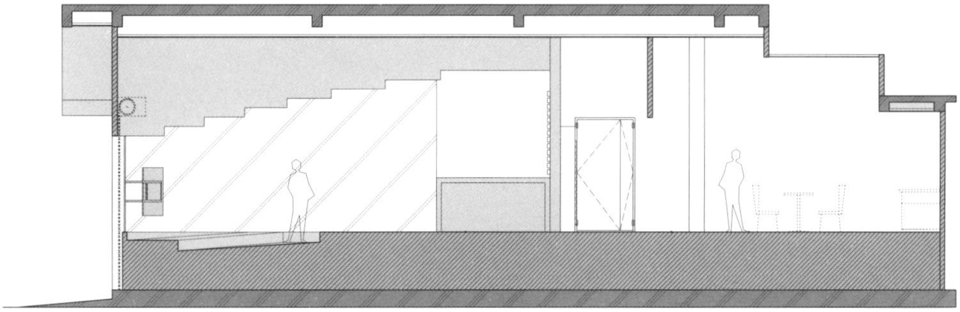

Section

Feeling the metamorphosis in the simplified design

- **Project name**
  Das Brot.
- **Location**
  Wolfsburg, Germany
- **Site area**
  1830 square feet
  (170 square meters)
- **Completion**
  2013
- **Interior design**
  Designliga GmbH & Co. KG
- **Photography**
  Designliga

The Autostadt restaurants are operated by a Swiss restaurant company Mövenpick. Mövenpick has been the partner of the Autostadt since its opening in 2000, and worked with the Autostadt to design and develop its catering concept. From 2003 onwards, all restaurants there began to move consistently to serving regional produce, the majority of which is grown or farmed according to ecological and seasonal principles. Organic certification is now the main criterion used in selecting suppliers. Transparency and regional sourcing are of the utmost importance for all foodstuffs used at the Autostadt.

Das Brot. was the logical continuation of this philosophy of regional, traditional onsite production, which permeates the restaurant concept there. After the ice-cream maker Cool and Creamy and homemade pasta restaurant La Coccinella, the bakery was the third food outlet to operate its own in-house production. All products served and sold at Das Brot. are 100 percent organic.

The sensory experience of seeing, touching, tasting, and feeling joins the basic philosophy of From Field to Counter—describing the value creation process involved in producing bread—to form the focus of the bakery's design, and the communication and perception of its image. The inclusion of traditional crafts and artisanal professions, such as mosaic and plasterwork artists and basket-weavers, is fundamental to the overall concept.

In the functional areas of the restaurant, the bakery and dining area flow into each other, creating a constantly changing ambient perspective. From the clean, clear lines of the workshop area to the homely familiarity of the

long table where guests sit down together, the feeling created by the restaurant space shifts and transforms. The patterns of the floor echo the bread-making process, in which a metamorphosis takes place from field to wheat, from wheat to flour and from flour—with water—to bread. The symbolic presentation of this creative process has both narrative and decorative value. At the same time, the floor design bears witness to an uncompromising quality of craftsmanship. Created in a partnership between traditional skills and modern computer technology, no two of the 25,000 elements of the floor are alike and all blend seamlessly into an overall image.

At the interface of tradition and the post-modern age, the interior design addresses independent traditional themes but eschews the contemporary trends so prevalent in Anglo-American coffee-house chains and French boulangeries. Instead, it references Central European coziness, reflected in the timber-framed style of the shelving and the plasterwork roof-tile impressions in the dining area ceiling, and teams these elements naturally and equally with the functional, almost clinical division of space. Lighting and acoustics are designed to be reminiscent of the cozy, safe feeling of a homely living room.

BUTTERBROT
BUTTERBROT
BUTTER BROT
WARM GERÖSTETES BROT
SAUERRAHMBUTTER
SAUERRAHMBUTTER
1.50
2.90
2.90
3.10
3.60
1.80

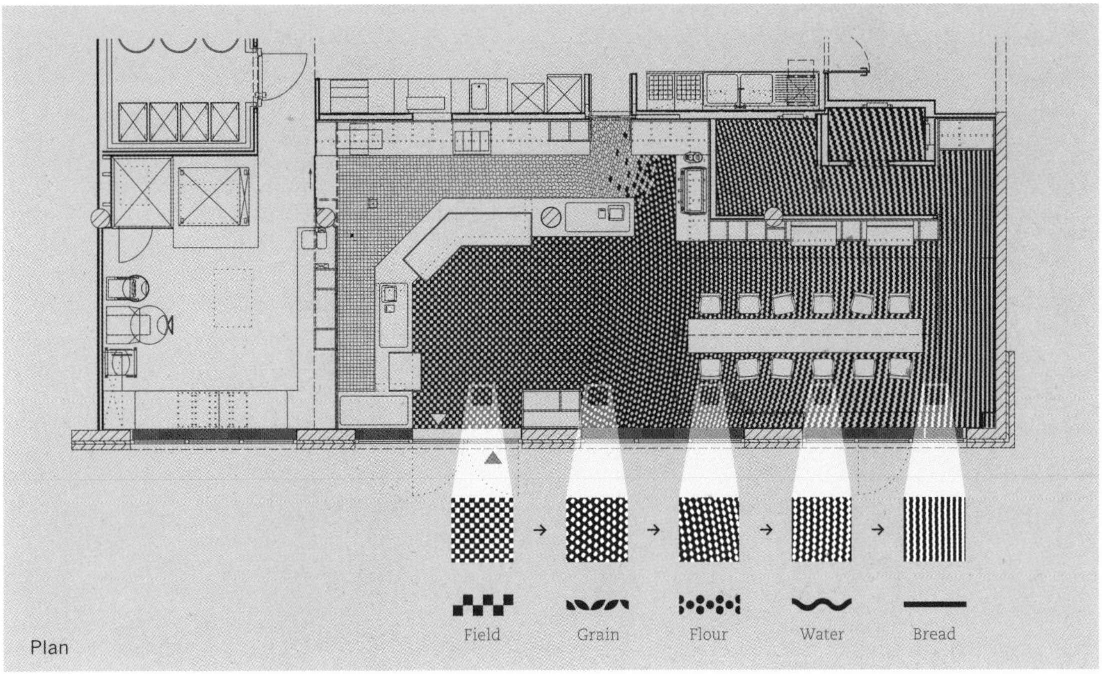

Plan

Fusion of French countryside and contemporary minimalism

- **Project name**
  Elysee
- **Location**
  Arta, Greece
- **Site area**
  1023 square feet
  (95 square meters)
- **Completion**
  2015
- **Interior design**
  G2LAB (George Efthymiadis, Giannis Efthymiadis)
- **Photography**
  Dimitris Spyrou

An old stone building, which is located in the center of Arta, a town in northwestern Greece, was the ideal place for the creation of a unique boulangerie patisserie. The space, with an almost double-the-average-ceiling height, had great visibility towards the street and was filled with abundant sunlight.

From the very beginning, the main design objective was the creation of an atmosphere that embodied characteristics of the bakeries in the French countryside, in combination with contemporary design features. The showcase of the products becomes an important element in the space, covered with an elaborate coating that resembles old trunks. The material textures were combined with the design forms and the light to reveal a creative game in the space. The grid of wooden beams on the ceiling discourses with the divider structure of the kitchen, which through its transparency enables the baking process to be visible from the main area.

Meanwhile, the surfaces in off-white hues result in the creation of a luxurious, minimalist space and serve as the appropriate background for the various, decorative items from different places and time periods. In addition, the wood on the floor is combined with tiles with geometrical patterns, while the black, metallic shelving and the pressed cement give a sense of industrial style. The furnishings in classic design are complementary to the decoration of the space.

The façade design complements the interior design perfectly. The solidity of the stone walls is disrupted by the big windows frames. The frame creates the necessary continuity between the interior and the surroundings. In other words, the inside comes closer to the urban life and the town square opposite, and the outside penetrates the inside space. The wooden frames of the windows in black color with the vertical grid and the blockboards create a geometrical game at the exterior elevation, adding intensity to the transparent layers of the windows.

The grey, metallic canopies, which are placed along the stone walls, protect the façades and enhance the industrial features. The smooth surfaces of metal and glass interact with the wood and the stone in a creative contrast, and result in a perfect balance of the whole

synthesis. The big openings of the two exterior elevations frame not only the design details, but also the products of the boulangeriepatisserie, creating a desire within the people passing by to taste them. The design of the display windows focuses on the installation of custom-made shelf units, made of metal and hanging from the ceiling, as well as on the right kind of lighting.

The lighting design has two distinctive goals. First, to highlight the architecture of the building and, second, to showcase the interior design and the goods. As for the exterior lighting design, downlight spots are placed on the metallic canopies, above the windows and in the corner of the building to highlight its architectural characteristics. Metallic lights with frosted glass were chosen to be placed on the stone walls, accentuating the construction grid.

The signage of the boulangerie patisserie is based on a minimal design, following the architectural design. Its dark color contrasts with the light-colored masonry, while at the same time its simple form respects the building architecture. The holistic approach of the design paying attention not only to the interior renovation, but also to the façades and the graphic design, results in a unique place. It combines different styles and characteristics in such a way that an organic whole is created.

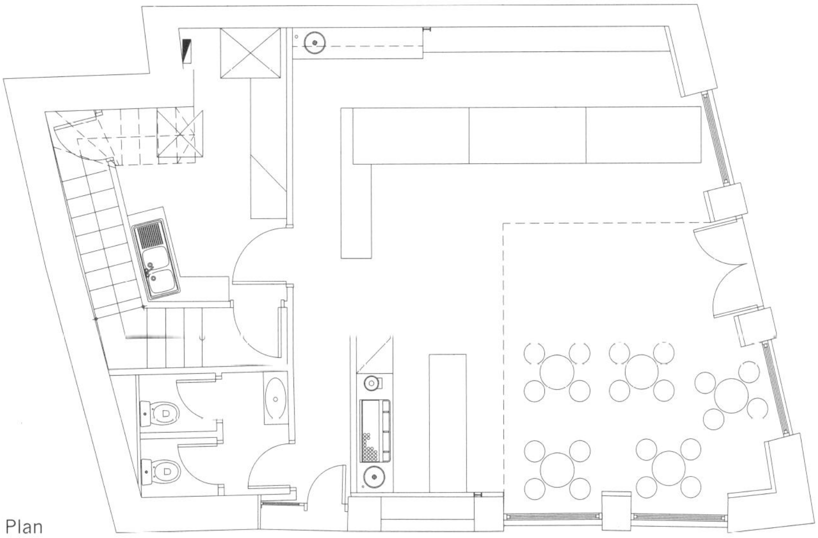

Plan

Collision between European taste and Japanese style

- **Project name**
  EZO Cheesecakes & Bakery
- **Location**
  Kelapa Gading Mall, North Jakarta, Indonesia
- **Site area**
  775 square feet (72 square meters)
- **Completion**
  2017
- **Interior design**
  Evonil Architecture
- **Photography**
  Evonil Architecture

This project sought to wed the classical yet elegant European-style bakery with the Japanese brand into the interior design, which was a challenging design task.

EZO Cheesecakes & Bakery specializes in creating delicious cheesecakes inspired from Hokkaido cheesecakes in Japan. The design challenge was to create a new and unique concept design for the bakery chain to lead the innovative and unique brand of the company by maintaining strong classical interior design elements with the authentic Japanese interior design character of the brand.

The combination between the classical interior design and Japanese interior design blend into one strong, original, and unique twist of interior design emphasized the usage of blue and mint finishes to upscale the feminine feel. Hence, the store offers a touch of classical design with a Japanese interior-design twist, made out of the solid-white pattern, bronze mirror, and wooden finishing carpentry with a mint finish on the wall.

Bright, clean, and clear lighting for the ceiling emphasizes the visual attractiveness from the entrance door and also accentuates the glass display of the main bakery goods. As additional decorative items at the wall, frames, and wall lamps complete and invigorate the touch of classical interior design.

For the customer seating area adjacent the counter, the long padded bench was fitted with blue fabric paired with rectangle tables of white Carrara marble. The walls were painted in a shade of mint creating character within the wall and the long rectangular spaces. The herringbone timber floor with two-tone color blends a luxurious and calm feeling into the design to create a united and warm atmosphere.

Plan

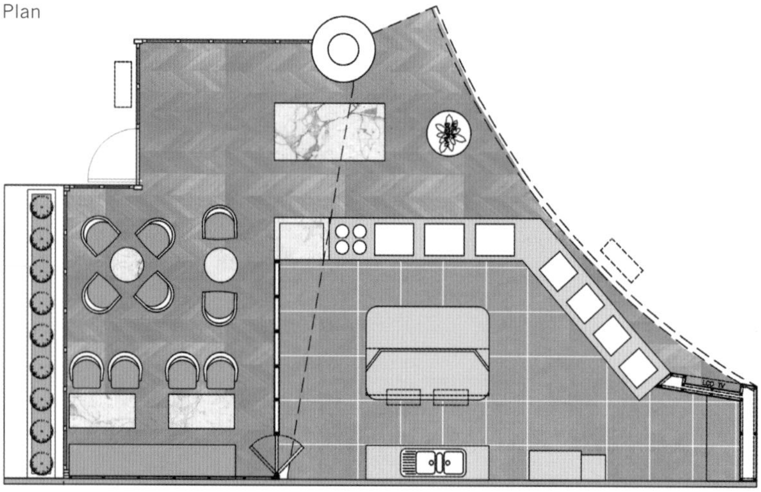

Section

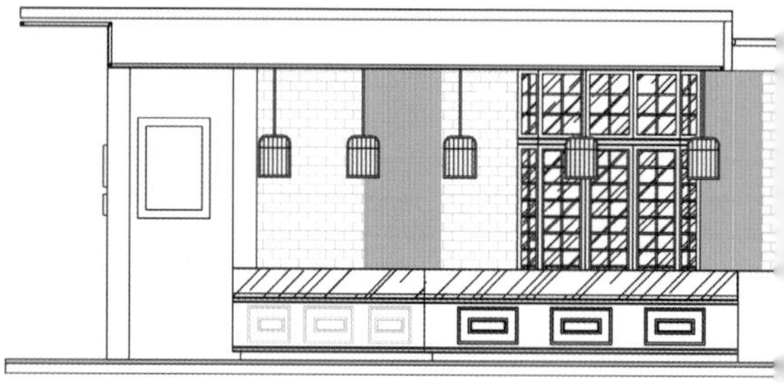

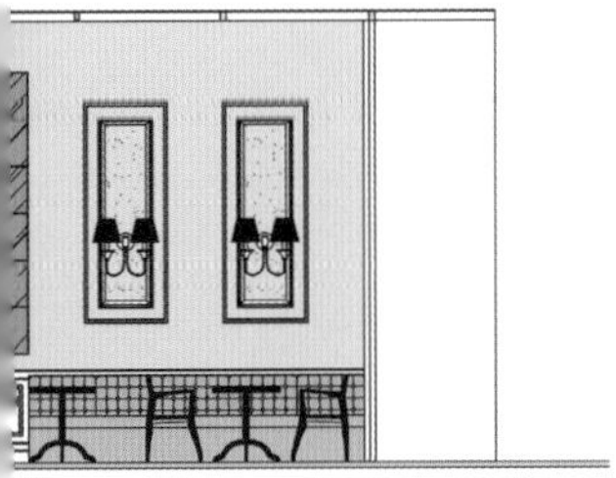

Natural, organic, and fresh

- **Project name**
  Fresco Banco & Cucina
- **Location**
  Milano, Italy
- **Site area**
  1776 square feet
  (165 square meters)
- **Completion**
  2016
- **Interior design**
  Margstudio
- **Photography**
  Sara Magni

Fresco Banco & Cucina was born from the desire to offer the public a new experience of healthy eating. It is located in the Scalo Milano City Style food court, a new shopping district in Milan dedicated to fashion, design, good food, and culture. They offer bread, cakes, salads, and gourmet sandwiches.

The project started from the idea of a greenhouse as a container of fresh and natural produce. The elements that make up the room are natural wood, darkened bronze, ceramics in texture (both covering and floor) glasses, and green colors. Everything was developed within the concept of nature: organic, fresh, and clean. The indoor space is in agreement with the produce concept. The food cabinet is displayed with small green plants, which can also be found hanging from the ceilings and walls. The dining tables are timber and the dining chairs are fresh green. The tableware is also in light green and white, giving a fresh and energetic feel to customers. In addition,

there are some seats for dining in front of the shop.

From a concept of fresh food and with an inside–outside greenhouse that provides a lot of ingredients in the store, it becomes an incubator for products sold fresh and freshly prepared. The vertical garden and back counter with fruit storage are watered daily by a micronized watering system to ensure freshness. The shop was designed with tones and textures that have a strong bond with the surrounding land, such as timber, light colors, handmade ceramics, and transparency. The interior design focuses on the integration of the brand, whether the color or the atmosphere. They are committed to giving customers a warm experience in every vibrant morning.

ALL THE TIME
Insalate
Salads

Panini
Sandwiches
PANCAKE

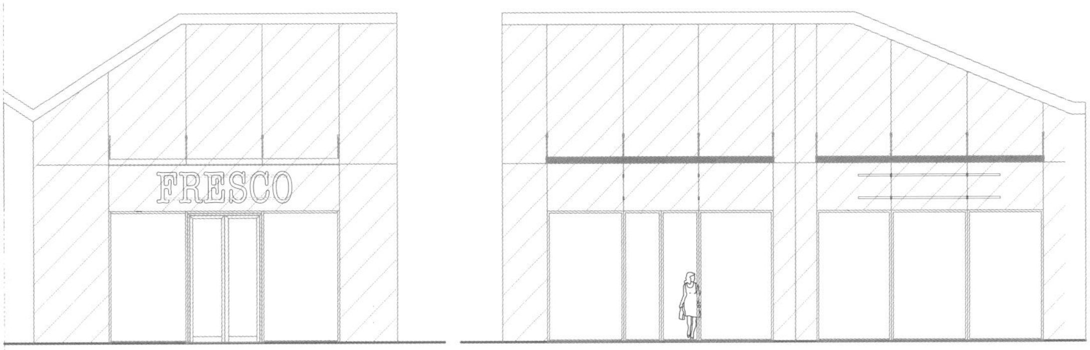

Section

MOLINARI

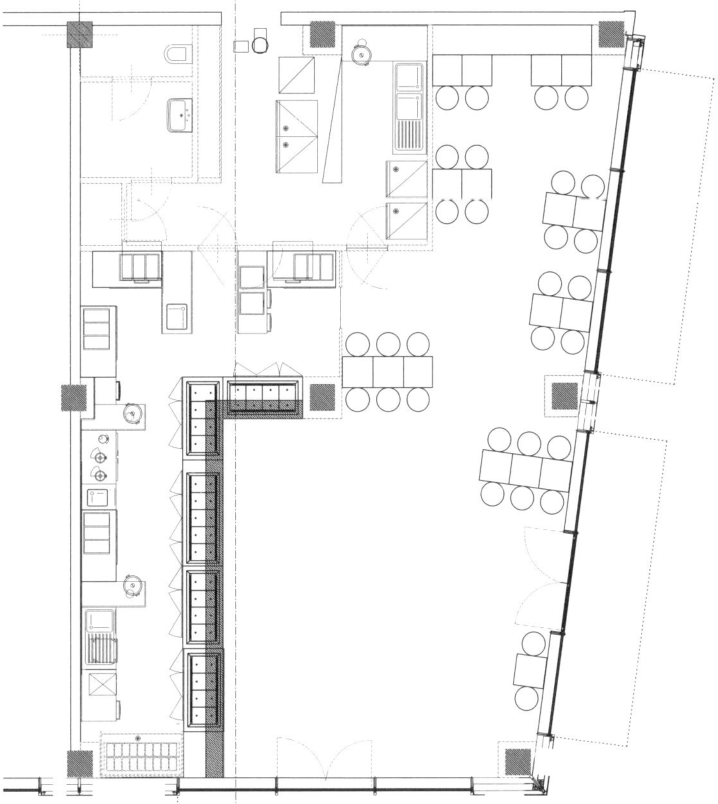

Plan

Pure space created by the white décor

- **Project name**
  Grandma Bakery Café—Nişantaşı
- **Location**
  Nişantaşı, Istanbul, Turkey
- **Site area**
  861 square feet
  (80 square meters)
- **Completion**
  2015
- **Interior design**
  Zemberek Design
- **Photography**
  Aytekin Demircioğlu

This bakery was the first in the Grandma branch by a new entrepreneur in the sector, offering a café bakery where traditional, natural, and organic products are sold. The shop supplies a variety of products such as sourdough breads, croissants, scones, bagels, muffins, different vegetable dishes, and cakes. The name "Grandma" was derived from the owner's grandmother, as her recipes brought the concept to life.

The aim was to create a warm, comfortable, and intimate environment—in sync with the "grandma" brand and the theme of the "neighborhood bakery"—yet working within an essentially sterile shop space. Additionally, the store had to have a way of keeping the products fresh every day and constantly rotating the products offered for sale at different times of the day.

In the design process, the product–customer relationship was re-evaluated in the approach, aspiring to give the products and the customers as close and unhindered a relationship as possible. In this context, it

was critical that the products be visible to passersby to showcase the products.

Another challenge was that the shop floor was lower than the street level, and it had a relatively low ceiling level. The solution was to make it easily visible from the inside and from the street, and to create an integrated outdoor-seating area that spilled off the interior of the shop.

To achieve this, the façade—which is also the shop window—was pulled back from the frontage of neighboring structures. Thus, the height of the façade increased and it became easier to perceive the interior from the outside. The middle part of the inside pocket was pulled towards the street so that the products could be easily observed from the outside, and the window space was increased. As such, the customers' spatial experience starts from the distance and continues without interruption to the products.

With the products as the foreground, the inviting, warm, and intimate space the

client wanted to create was achieve through materials, textures, and color choices. The whites help to create a clean and holistic look. Familiar and warm materials such as solid wood and ceramics further bolster this warmth. The handmade aging-brass-iron details also promote the brand identity.

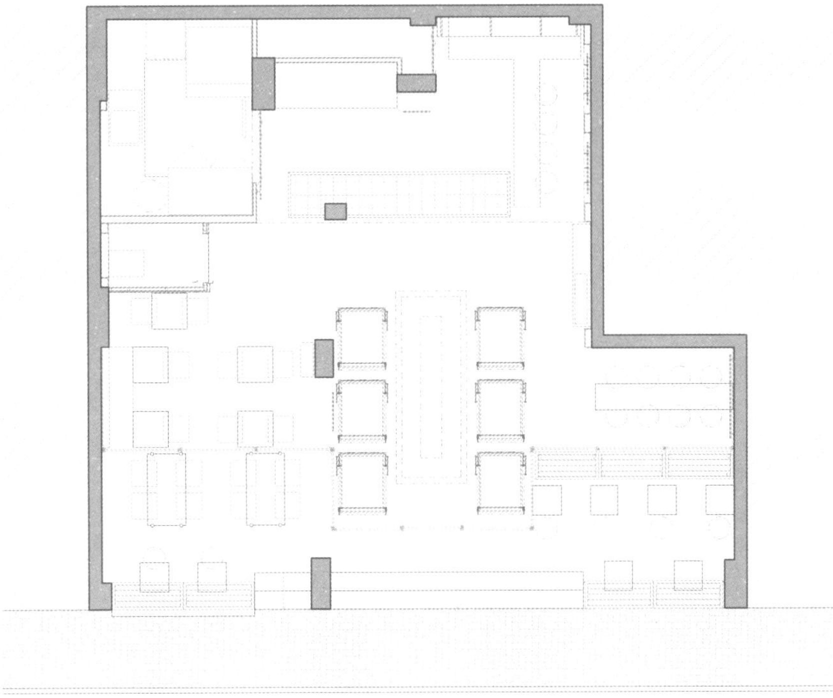

Plan

Warm environment created by white patterns and materials

- **Project name**
  Grandma Bakery Café—Akmerkez
- **Location**
  Akmerkez Shopping Mall, Etiler, Istanbul, Turkey
- **Site area**
  2583 square feet (240 square meters)
- **Completion**
  2017
- **Interior design**
  Zemberek Design
- **Photography**
  Safak Emrence

The second store of the Grandma brand is an artisan café bakery that offers products that are made the natural, organic, and traditional way. As mentioned in the previous case study, the name "Grandma" was derived from the owner's grandmother, as her recipes brought the concept to life.

The brand's design story started with its first store, which had a design concept of a "neighborhood bakery." After coming up with the idea of opening a branch in a shopping mall, the necessity of merging the coexistence of these two different concepts—which have cultural contradictions in their roots—became apparent. As such, the aim was for the store to be able to bring itself into existence in the shopping mall's sterilized, active, and consumption-oriented dynamics in its own way that melds with the grandmother concept, which is cozy, comfortable, protected, and sincere in spatial sensation.

The grandmother concept, which underlies in brand's story, is reflected in the design of

the place, which has a wide outdoor space. The concepts of sincerity, comfort, experience, multilayeredness, and good memories reminiscent of being in grandmother's backyard is infused into the atmosphere of the space.

Effective criteria in materials, color, and pattern selections were not only for the sense of professionalism of the brand in the store but also the sustainability of a warm and inviting atmosphere when the products stand out. Dominance of white in different patterns and materials used in the store formed the basis of the atmosphere in points of matching up with the brand's corporate identity and supporting the integrated construct. As warm and familiar materials like solid wood and ceramic refer to the warm identity of the store, handmade and distressed brass details were used for supporting the brand's artisan attitude. In sitting areas, different furniture and fabrics were used together to arouse the feeling of spontaneity and life experience. Most of the furniture was specially designed for the store and readymade furniture was picked from secondhand stores.

Along with its outdoor space, Grandma Bakery Café has an interior space where there are exhibition units of various products and brands in the shopping mall. The interior space is separated from shopping mall's common

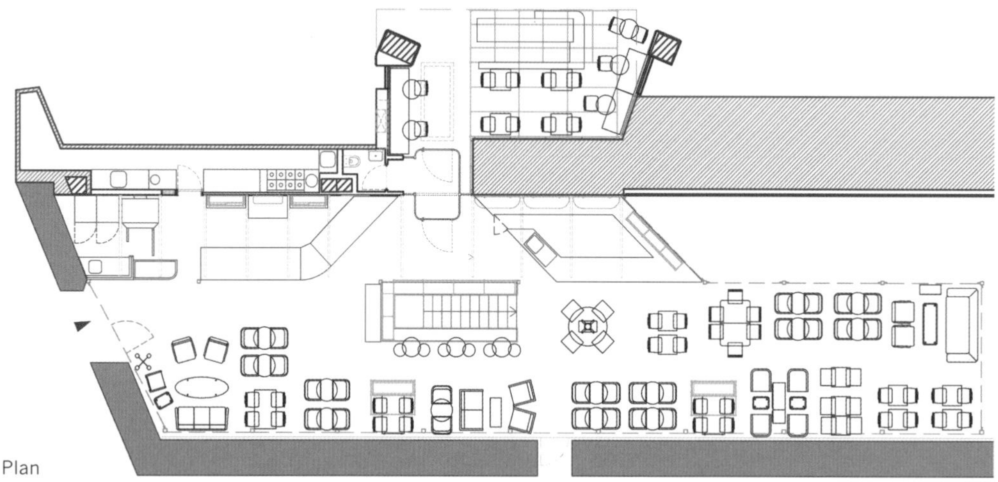

Plan

areas in a permeable way with a light structural shell. In the outdoor space, due to administrative necessities, the counter and service area are located under eaves that complete the shopping mall's volume. For the purpose of defining the space, a structural covering component, composed of metal, was placed under the eaves.

The transit area that connects the bakery's interior and exterior space is located between the bar and service area in a way that will not interrupt the sustainability of the relationship between the customer and product.

All day breakfast
Specialty Coffee
Cakes & Tarts
Daily Fresh Pastries
grandma
BYREDO

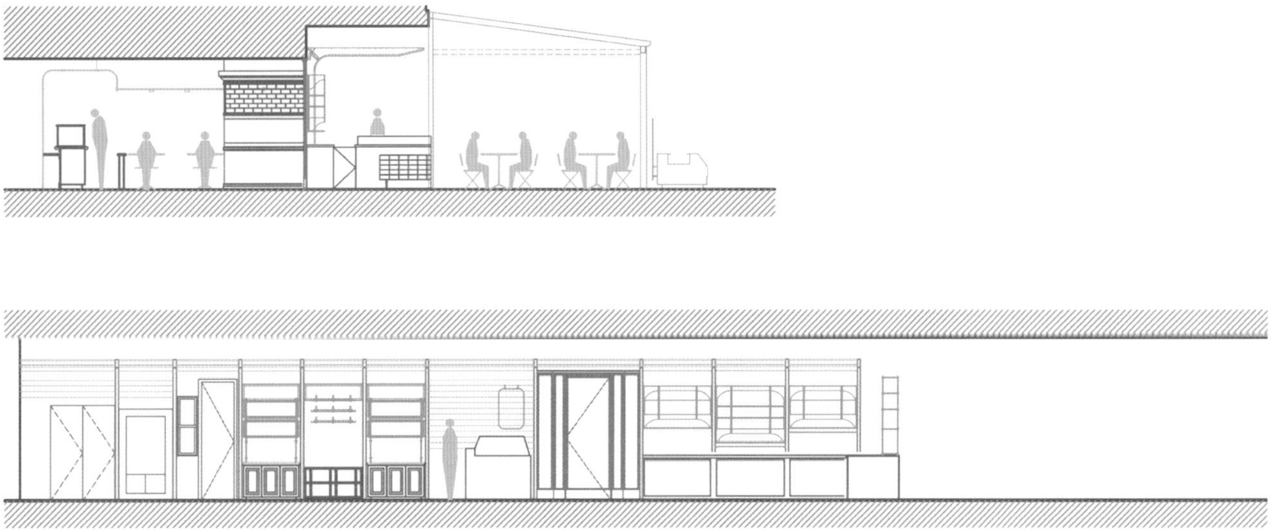

Sections

Splicing art of planks and concrete

- **Project name**
  GUMASSIF/WITH Sanlitun Bakery in Beijing
- **Location**
  Beijing, China
- **Site area**
  1615 square feet
  (150 square meters)
- **Completion**
  2016
- **Interior design**
  B.L.U.E. Architecture Studio
- **Photography**
  Ruijing Photo

Located beside a street in southern Taikoo Li in Sanlitun, Beijing, B.L.U.E. Architecture Studio was tasked with designing the interior and façade of the Withwheat bakery. Creating a façade made of a full-height glass curtain wall, people can look in at the warm interiors defined by white and solid-wood framework.

The highlight of this design is a framework made from solid wood, which extends from ground to ceiling. To create complexity as well as keep a sense of rhythm, the vertical wooden stripes attached to the ceiling are different lengths. A bread display case is placed in the center, which breaks the holistic design of this full-height framework. The customized solid-wood frame is not only environmentally friendly, but also has a very good decorative effect and reflects the natural characteristics of the bread while drawing in the eyes of the customers.

A concrete wall works with old flanks, which are spliced together into the shape

of wheat. The image of wheat changes gradually from below to above, until it disappears. These wheat-shaped ornaments nicely echo the theme of the bakery. In order to create an uneven surface, the background wall behind the counter is composed of old flanks with different thickness. As a consequence of using gray concrete bricks and stainless-brass stripes, the ground is delicate and rich.

No matter from what aspect the space is viewed, the layout, material, and lighting of the interior of this bakery emanates a warm, refreshing, and pure ambience.

Plan

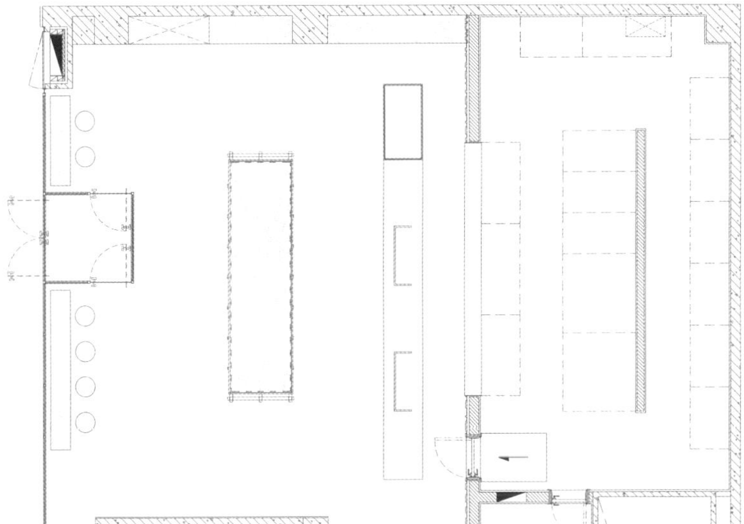

Space wrapped by semicircular translucent paper

- **Project name**
  The White Gift Box
- **Location**
  Huangpu District, Shanghai, China
- **Site area**
  678 square feet (63 square meters)
- **Completion**
  2014
- **Interior design**
  Lukstudio
- **Photography**
  Peter Dixie for LOTAN Architectural Photography

Aimé Pâtisserie, a new brand entering the Shanghai market, positioned its flagship store in an elevated retail strip on Huai Hai Road. The chosen site is flanked by familiar coffee and donut franchises, and fronted by a city bus stop. Across the street is the recently opened shopping mall flaunting an array of luxury brands. The design challenge of the store was to make it stand out from its immediate chaos and appeal to the clientele from the close-by gentrified neighborhood. The solution was to dress this newcomer up as a white gift box.

The unwrapping experience of the Aimé gift box is translated into the physical store. The idea of layering appears when designers lift one semicircular translucent paper after another to discover the colorful macarons within. This opening sequence gives form to the overhead storefront design, while the window display made of four translucent layers attracts passersby to explore inside the store.

Beyond the 14.76-foot (4.5-meter) retail storefront lies a turning L-shape layout

divided into two zones: the foyer with bar seating and the display counter at the back. With a lower ceiling, the former compresses views of the latter, yet frames the illuminated feature wall to capture the curious minds. Every step forward heightens the discovery of the playful interior where the 29.5-foot-long (9-meter-long) counter showcases macarons and other goodies in perfect order.

The illuminated feature wall composed of stacked gift boxes at various states of opening draws one's eyes up to the ceiling were the whimsical pattern continues. The versatile modular system allows for necessary wall display shelves, and ceiling openings for spotlights, speakers, and security devices.

In light of the neutral palette evoking a gallery ambiance, the branding wall is created with an artistic approach where aluminum bands are twirled and bent to cast calligraphic shadow. A visit to this white gift box should be a delight to the eyes as much as to the sweet tooth.

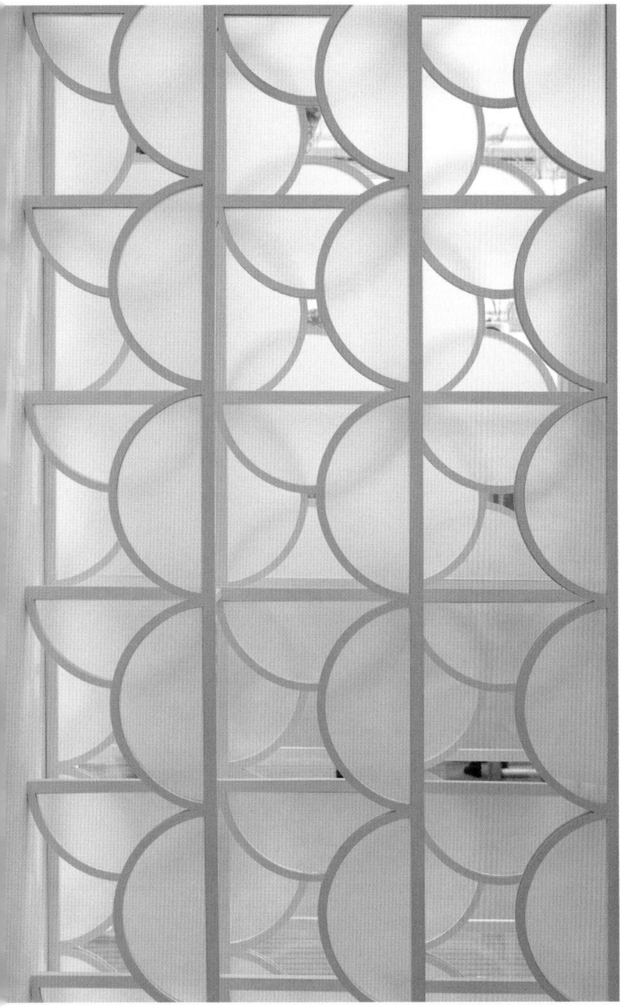

AIMÉ PÂTISSERIE

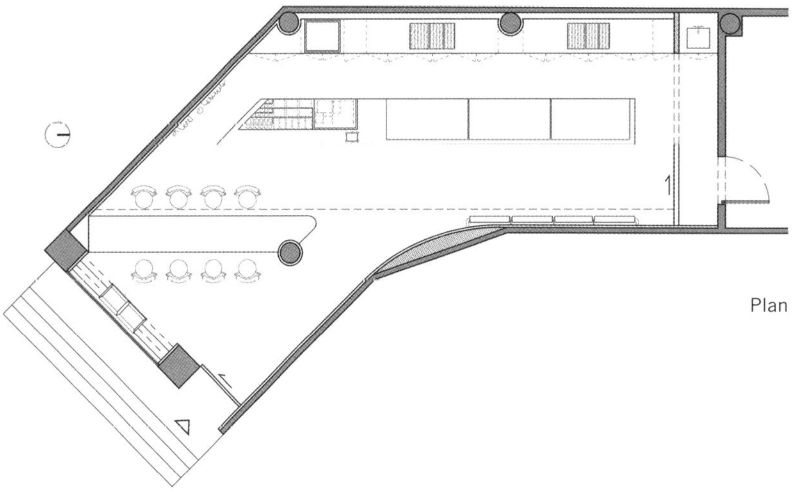

Plan

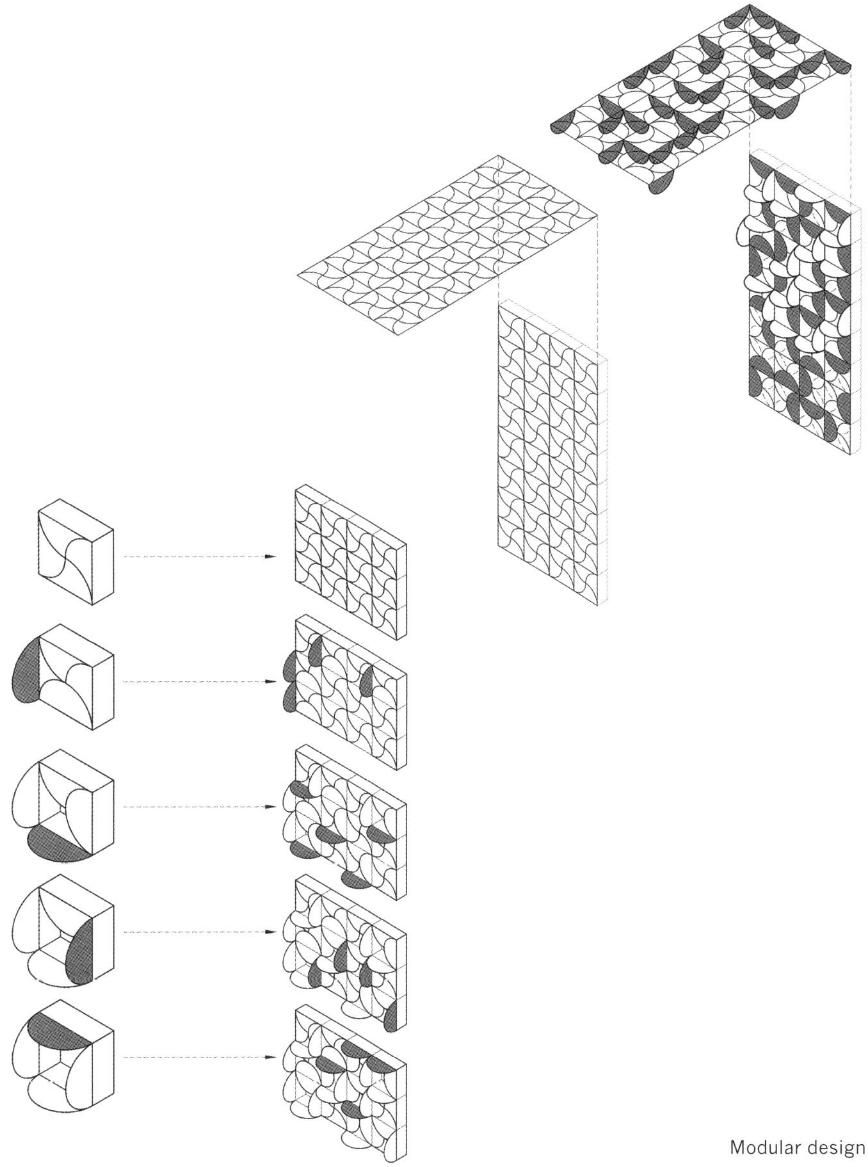

Modular design

Unified stainless-steel style

- **Project name**
  Kerry Centre Store of Mr. Maimai
- **Location**
  Kerry Centre, Hangzhou,China
- **Site area**
  484 square feet (45 square meters)
- **Completion**
  2016
- **Interior design**
  Hangzhou AN Interior Design Co.,Ltd.
- **Photography**
  Liu Yujie

Situate in the Kerry Centre shopping mall in Hangzhou, the designers created an all-metal bakery. This striking stainless-steel space provides an excellent marker for people lost in the shopping mall.

The space is a semi-arc, its two sides are wide open, and it's about 484 square feet (45 square meters). The fire hydrant and load-bearing on one side is 6.56 feet (2 meters) wide and 2.95 feet (0.9 meter) long. The slant load-bearing sticks on the top face the escalator directly. The key design point of Mr. Maimai was to form a visual focus around the pillar and express the space implicitly by covering the pillar.

The special counter hidden in the pillar extends to the whole space. The section of the single-glass breadbox adopted the black screen print to keep the bread fresh and keep its attractive color and luster.

The dining area is totally open and arranged like a school desk. All the guests face one direction, to keep the dining

process interesting. All visual expression is neat and straight while also being continuous and metabolic.

The whole space is made of brushed stainless-steel only. The main light hidden in the construction and the light source covered by acrylic gave the brushed stainless-steel a gentle luster.

Plan

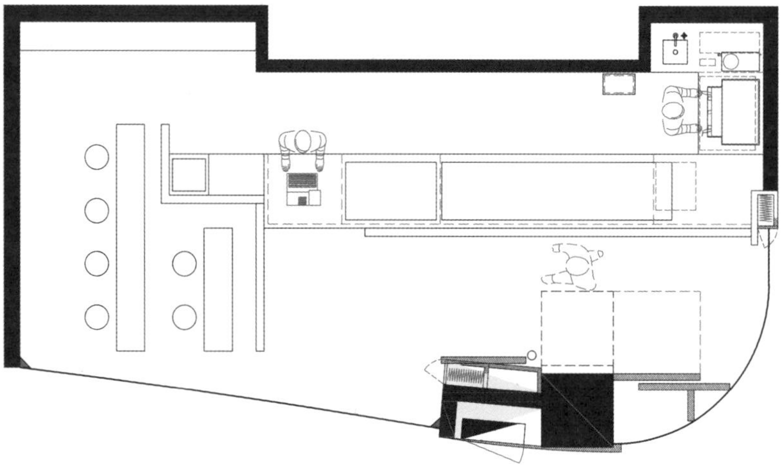

Dining experiences under the tree shade

- **Project name**
  Pantry's Best—the Tree
- **Location**
  Shanghai, China
- **Site area**
  570 square feet
  (53 square meters)
- **Completion**
  2015
- **Interior design**
  Lukstudio architects
- **Photography**
  Peter Dixie for LOTAN Architectural Photography

This project is located in a shopping mall in Shanghai. In such a prosperous area, in order to create a store identity for a cupcake brand, the Lukstudio architects thought one common ground between finishing a cupcake and an interior could be the idea of sculpting.

Inspired by a bird drawing in the brand's visual graphics, the architects decided to give the little bird a cute tree dwelling, and the customers a comfortable "under the shade" experience. Having chosen the tree form as the subject of the sculptural experiment, they required the negotiation between the idea, the pragmatic retail requirements, and the site-specific constraints.

Given a big column in the middle of the 570-square-foot (53-square-meter) basement booth, Lukstudio transformed the spatial obstacle into a sculptural opportunity: a huge tree trunk extending from the ground and expanding into a sinuous foliage inspired by the cupcake

icing. Peepholes perforate the tree trunk, giving the impression of traces left by woodpeckers. They invoke childlike curiosity in passersby, inviting them to peek inside for some hidden treasure.

The bespoke table collection—"Twiggy"—mimics the rustic idea of using light tree branches to support a timber top for use. "Twigs" branch out at the end of the legs to become corner hooks for bags. The square and quadrant shapes allow flexible grouping under the tree, a new mall concept renowned for integrating art and commerce, the "tree" idea molds into another form in the small booth. Resembling elongated willow tree branches, wooden cylinders are suspended from the ceiling in different densities and lengths, forming a foliage-like sculpture above the retail display. Sitting on the white counter, these wooden cylinders become display plinths for the brand's signature desserts. It is easy for customers to feel comfortable when in a clean and welcoming under-a-tree environment.

Step4
Step1

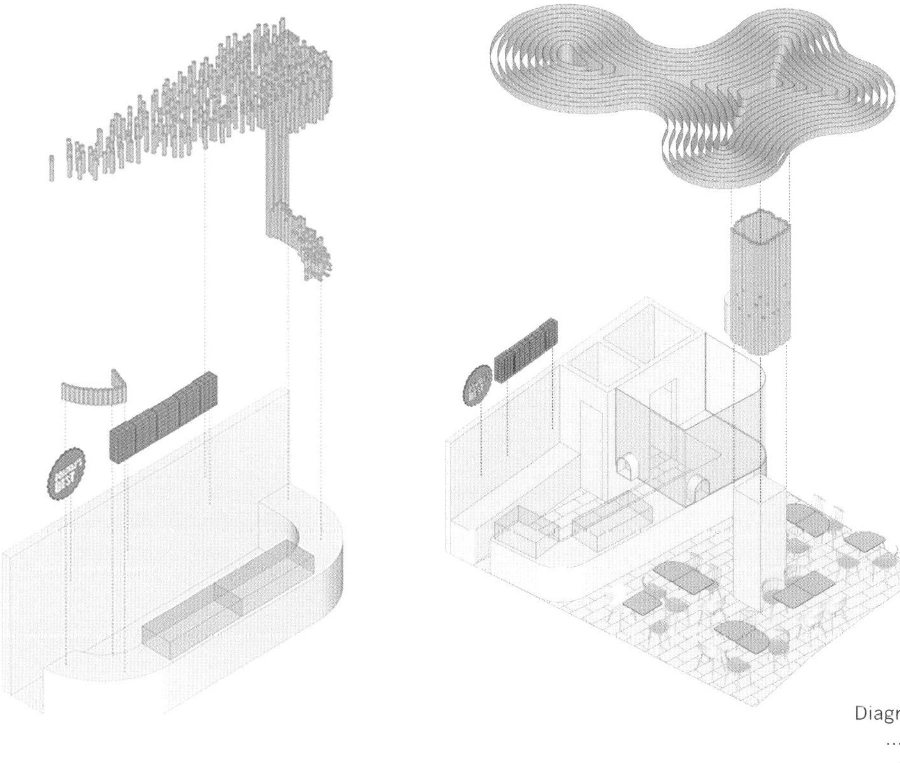

Diagram

Nostalgia style emitting an exotic atmosphere

- **Project name**
  Binario 11
- **Location**
  Milano, Italy
- **Site area**
  1615 square feet
  (150 square meters)
- **Completion**
  2013
- **Interior design**
  Andrea Langhi Design
- **Photography**
  Daniele Domenicali

Binario 11, designed by Andrea Langhi Design, is home to the main train station within 10 tracks in Milan. The venue is situated in an old mansion and it is divided into two different areas: the bakery and the dining room.

The bakery space is adorned with hanging Renaissance reproductions from Agnolo Bronzino with a floor created with the best Italian Intarsia method. A black back wall with poems from Giovanni Pascoli explaining the process of making bread merges with the original structural bricks and industrial lighting to create a whole new way of displaying food, celebrating the wholesomeness of Italian bakeries. Surrounded by décor evoking passion for the beautiful, customers can not only enjoy the bakery food in this space, but also feel the classical culture of Italy.

The dining space is a bit more romantic, evoking a nostalgia of the Orient Express era. The floor is a black-and-white chessboard and there is a clever mixture of

styles, becoming even a bit exotic. The bar has an old distressed look with a pewter top. There is a mezzanine level with tables and chairs overlooking the ground floor where the guests can appreciate the scale of the big round lanterns illuminating the space. The mezzanine area is relatively quiet and guests can savor the food and relax.

The counter is constructed over old suitcases in sync with the romantic "journey" theme of and train travel, referring to a vaguely exotic atmosphere with a mixture of styles and different influences. Memories almost completely forgotten are resurfaced in this space behind the Cadorna railway station, which has 10 tracks, making Binary 11 a fictional track that exists only in fantasy.

Plan

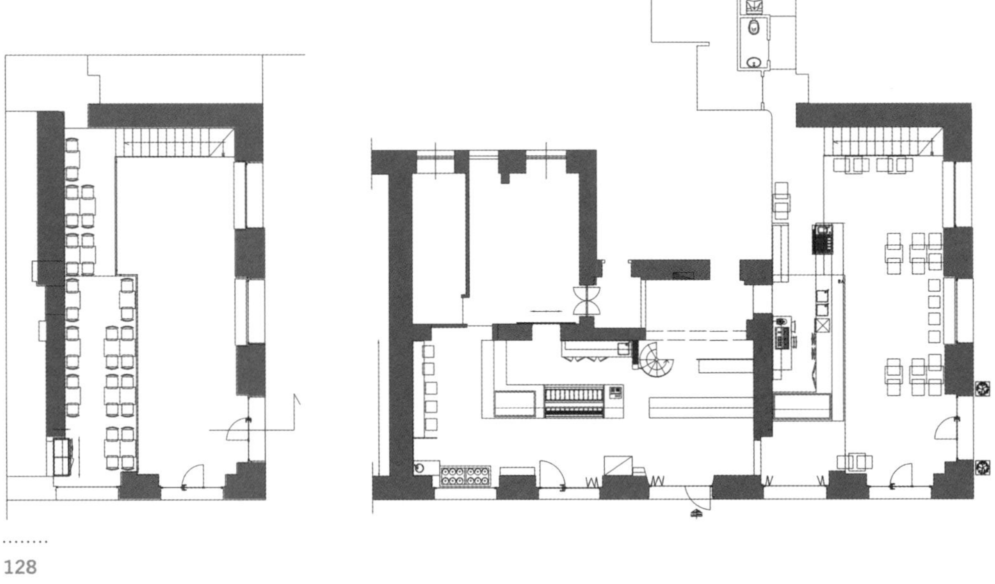

Exposed walls and red bricks

- **Project name**
  Heritage Bakery & Café
- **Location**
  Taipei, Taiwan, China
- **Site area**
  1765 square feet
  (164 square meters)
- **Completion**
  2016
- **Interior design**
  J.C. Architecture
- **Photography**
  Zach Hone

A residential building passed on from generation to generation was the chosen site for the Heritage Bakery & Café by owner Sally Song. The street had become a hub for camera and gadget-like retailers as the neighborhood revitalized, creating a destination for young travelers and students to meet up. As such, the designers aimed to open the shop to invite in the new stream of customers.

Inspired by the height and narrowness of the site, the designers envisioned the space as an alleyway, a continuation of the streetscape in Taipei city, aiming to recapture the traces of the building's history, purposely exposing its bare walls full of red bricks and tiles to the space to reveal the old-time beauty to the present.

In reference to the outdoor farmer's market and its daily preparations, the designers inserted a vending stall-like structure within a wooden box, as crates are used to deliver the fresh goods. In reference to the contemporary neighborhood—

surrounded by camera shops—they used industrial details such as metal structures overlapping each other, giving a depth perception of a viewfinder. Tables were hung along the wall as street light posts, while a long family-style table bridges over the void that links the first and second floor. Along the void designers added a vertical mural, a concrete layer to display future artist works and the bakery's daily special.

Engaging a combination of traditional and industrial style in high contrast with new and modern materials, Heritage Bakery & Café is an American-style dessert shop with attitude. The alley-like space becomes a pleasant stop for quick meals, coffee, or small gatherings. The memories passed through the generations in the building have been integrated into a timeless and beautiful space.

Second-floor plan

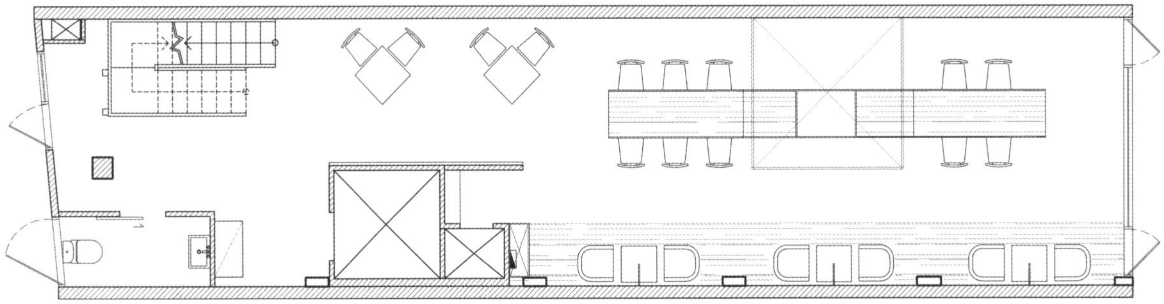

First-floor plan

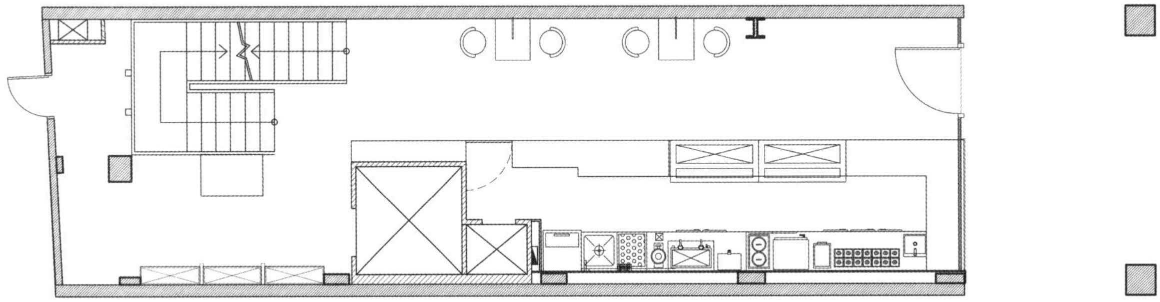

HERITAGE

HERITAGE
Bakery and Cafe

HERITAGE

時代大樓

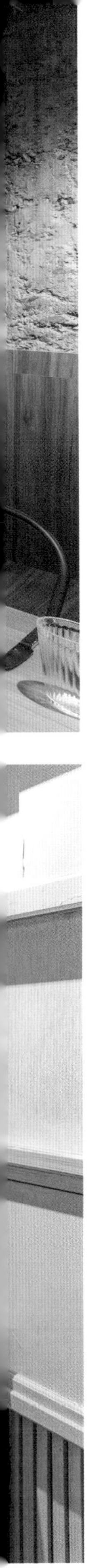

Transplant of traditional Indian materials

- **Project name**
  Kushino No Panya
- **Location**
  Chiba, Japan
- **Site area**
  484 square feet
  (45 square meters)
- **Completion**
  2016
- **Interior design**
  Hand&Design (Tetsuya Furukawa), Rungta.co.,ltd (Nozomi Haga)
- **Photography**
  Nozomi Haga

Kushino No Panya opened in 2016 in the newly developed residential area. The concept of the design was to create a beloved, long-lasting shop, so the designers focused on using sustainable natural materials, working with artisans in India.

In India, there are still many artisans who use the same traditional techniques of several hundred years ago, yet these traditions are vanishing in Japan. Japanese designers have a deep respect for the time-consuming and intricate work of these artisans, so they went to India to select traditional old woods and sustainable natural materials, which can be traced from production to distribution.

The designers eliminated plastics and plywoods as much as possible, replacing them with these natural materials, as they wanted to create a warm and environmentally-friendly environment. This theme works in harmony with the fresh, handmade bread the bakery produces.

To make the 1.57-inch (4-centimeter) thick marble tops and floor tiles, the designers found a 282.5-cubic-foot (8-cubic-meter) marble block to hew out the pieces one by one, after quality checking to unify the vein within the stone. The pieces were used for the traditional bar counter, table, and flooring tile. The vintage teak door opening to the kitchen is about 150 years old and the original size was over 9.8 feet (3 meters). Designers also reused old timber cut from pillar and beams for shelving and furniture. These woods were sourced from the old Maharaja Palace and residences.

As for lighting, the designers asked local traditional artisans for wood turning to make the parts from these woods. All productions were hand done by artisans because they were not able to mass-produced and the work is time consuming. The owner and the designers paved the marble flooring themselves to understand the hard work of Indian artisans. The designers maintained a focus on processes throughout, not the detail.

Plan

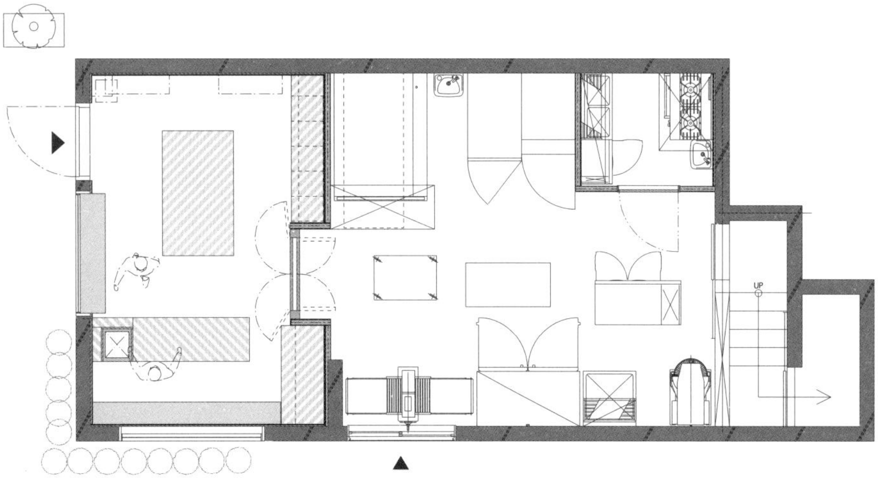

Sections

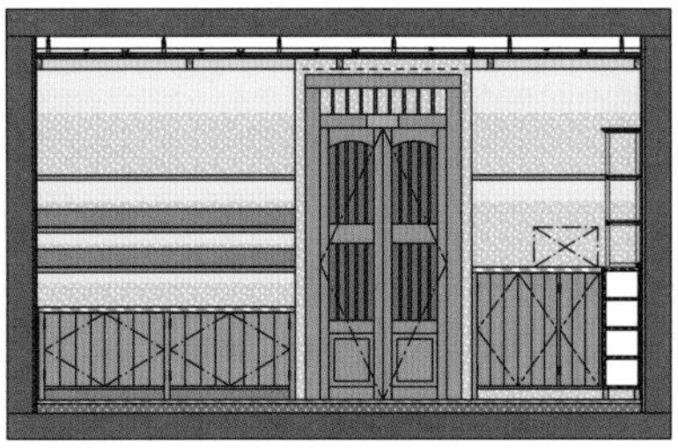

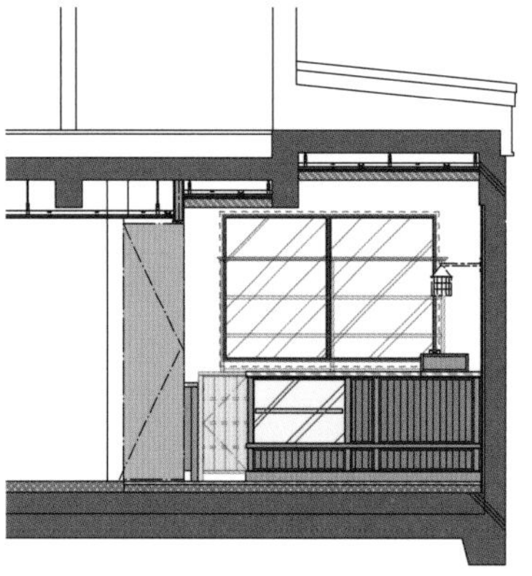

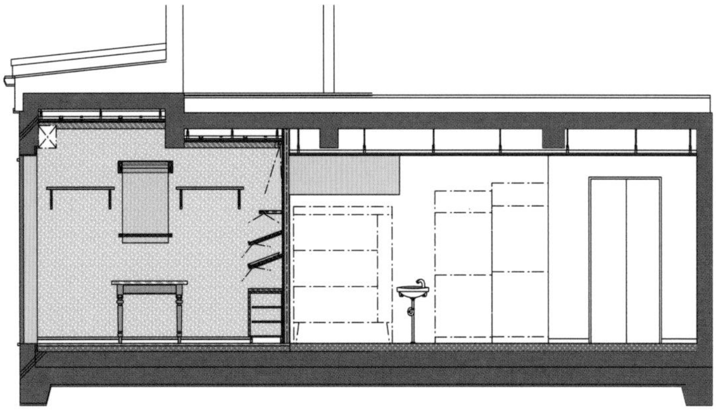

"Black" sweet

- **Project name**
  Manteigaria—Custard Tart Bakery
- **Location**
  Lisbon, Portugal
- **Site area**
  753 square feet
  (70 square meters)
- **Completion**
  2016
- **Interior design**
  DC.AD
- **Photography**
  Francisco Nogueira

Manteigaria is a custard tart bakery located in the Ribeira Market in Lisbon. The site covers an area of 753 square feet (70 square meters), within the perimeter of the Timeout Market, laid out according to the plan designed by Francisco Aires Mateus. The logic of continuity established by the aforementioned architect incorporated the utilization of predefined finishing materials rendering obligatory the application of black wall tiles and Lioz marble stone for the counters and working surfaces.

The concept established for Manteigaria revolved around the design of a space that is made up of the two stores existing in the market, which were not formerly interconnected. Based upon this premise, designers created a single space with two storefronts—one facing towards the market interior and the other opening onto the adjoining 24 de Julho Avenue, with an interlinking and shared space given over to the production of the custard tarts. This central area is separated from the two sales points by glass divisions so that

clients may observe the ongoing cake-making process. These glass partitions also enable a frank and transparent relationship to develop between the interior and exterior environments of the market and underpinning the perception of this as a single, unique place.

For the storefront facing 24 de Julho Avenue, the objective was to design a central counter for serving the public, which directly interlinked the bakery with the exterior through the two existing windows. These windows were adapted to allow for them to be mechanically opened outwards providing for product sales in a takeaway format. This also extended to a space for clients with an eating counter located in the store interior.

For the market interior, the concept adopted the grab-and-go format and thus incorporating only two counters facing towards the interior of the food-court similar to the other outlets in the market.

The store ambience was inspired by the constructive logic of the traditional, existing market, making recourse to constructions made out of black metallic structures, whether fixed or mobile, finished in the glass and stone panels, which divide up the three distinct moments of the store. Despite the obligation to utilize the core finishing materials, there was also the introduction of new materials able to nurture a distinctive environment for the space, in particular the panels in Tinos green marble that punctually introduce new textures and splashes of color.

A purpose-designed suspended chandelier was also installed to emphasize the ceiling height while making reference to a classical language with a contemporary constructive logic, seeking to reach out to the intervention project principles that rest upon achieving an equilibrium between a contemporary intervention and this historical location within the city.

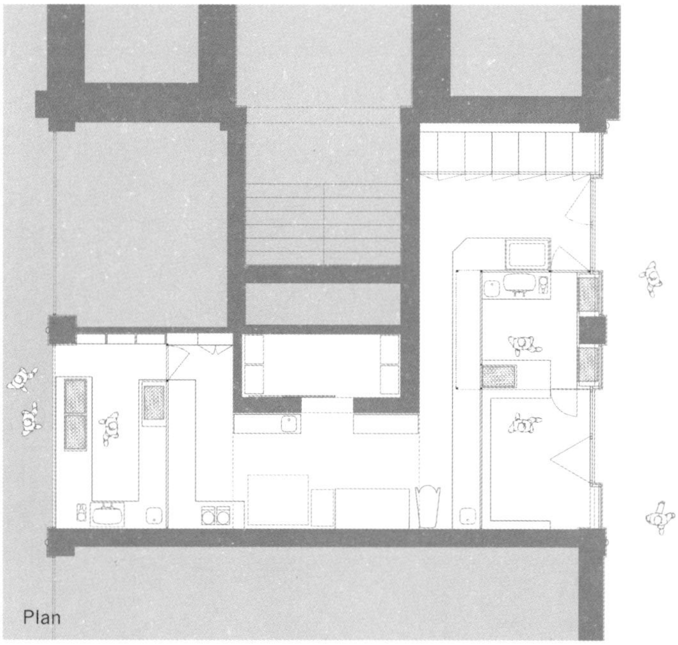

Plan

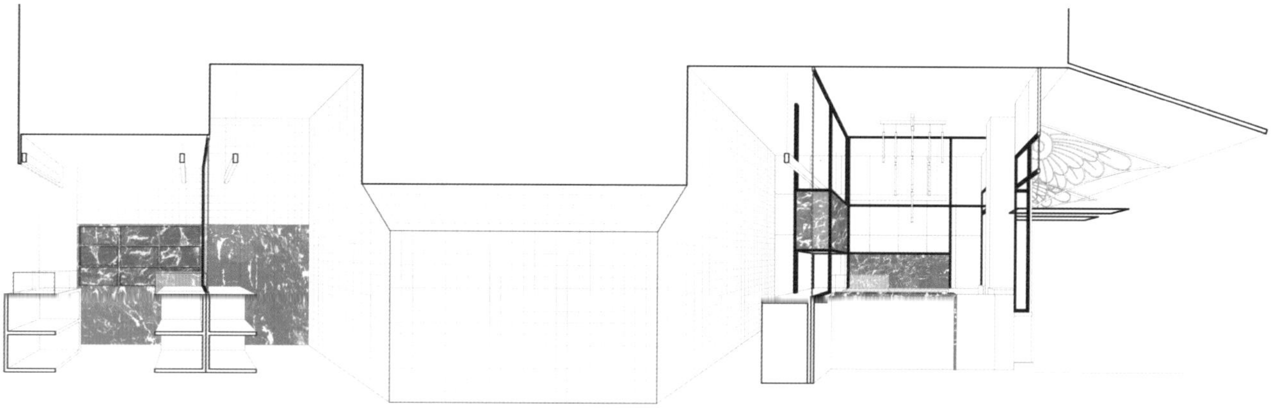

Section

Bubble space comprising cedar wood spheres

- **Project name**
  Omonia Bakery
- **Location**
  Queens, New York, United States
- **Site area**
  1200 square feet (111 square meters)
- **Completion**
  2012
- **Interior design**
  bluarch (Antonio Di Oronzo, Masashi Kobayashi)
- **Photography**
  Oleg March

This bakery was a brand-new project for the family behind the renowned Omonia brand, famous for its Greek pastries. It sells pastries and breads prepared on the premises in the see-through kitchen.

The design of this store celebrates indulgence, the pause in one's everyday grind to stop and savor a sweet delight. The space is soft and warm, sexy and decadent, like chocolate. The design sought to emulate the exciting anticipation of awaiting a sweet cake or pastry. The space itself shifts organically with the variety of flavors as patrons browse—and taste!—the succulent goods.

The main feature of the 1000-square-foot (93-square-meter) interior space is a fluid surface clad with ¼-inch (0.64-centimeter) chocolate-brown tiles. This surface covers the ceiling and the side walls to different heights. The shape of the ceiling was modeled in 3D and fabricated with a CNC milling machine to obtain smooth curvatures and transitions.

The outcome was complex geometry that could only be accommodated with very small tiles, which were sourced from the Italian high-end brand Bisazza. These were installed by Italian artisans who traveled from Southern Italy for this project. As the ceiling surface warps in bubbles, it negotiates a system of 6-inch (15-centimeter) tubular incandescent light bulbs and an arrangement of red-cedar wood spheres. The lights emanate a soft, warm-white glow and are placed between the chocolate-brown surface and the cedar spheres. The epoxy flooring continues to the walls via filleted corners. A shelf and LED strips navigate the transition with the chocolate surface.

The kitchen is exhibited to the public, as it sits simply within a tempered glass box. As such, the exquisite level of craftsmanship of the project (with its unforgiving alignments and complex details) is paralleled with the refined artisanship of Omonia's pastries. The overall results are self-evidently outstanding.

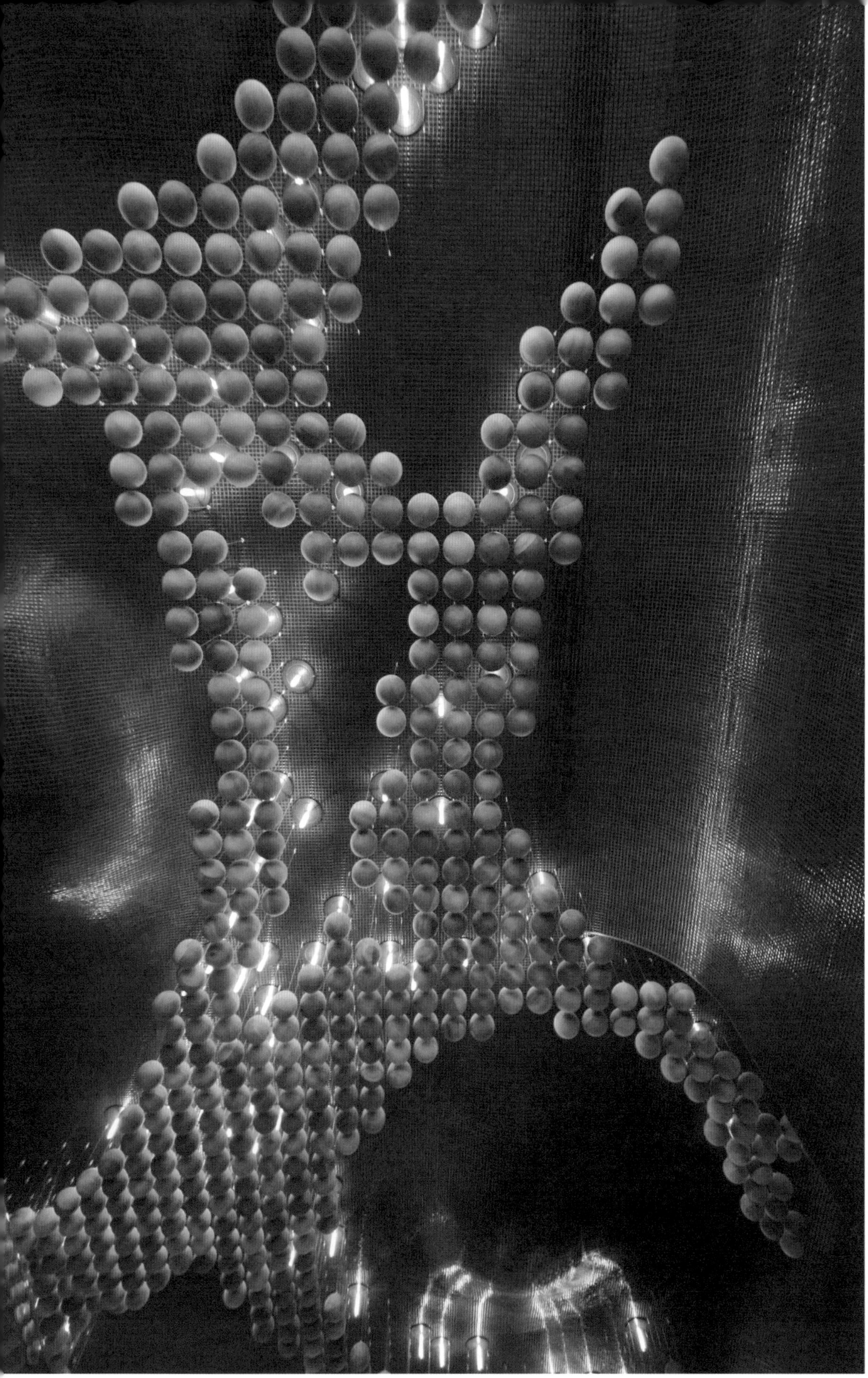

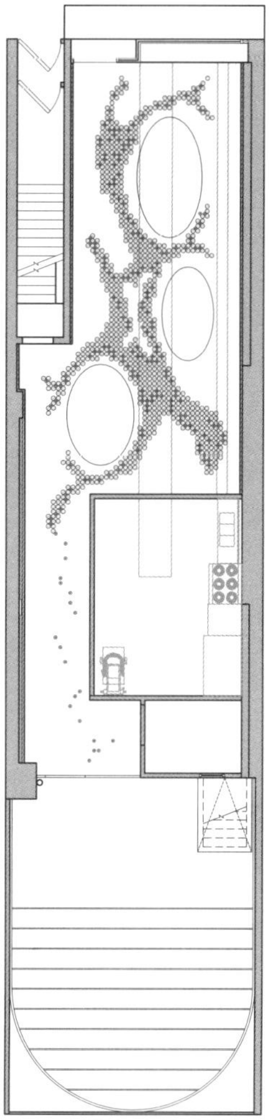

Ceiling plan

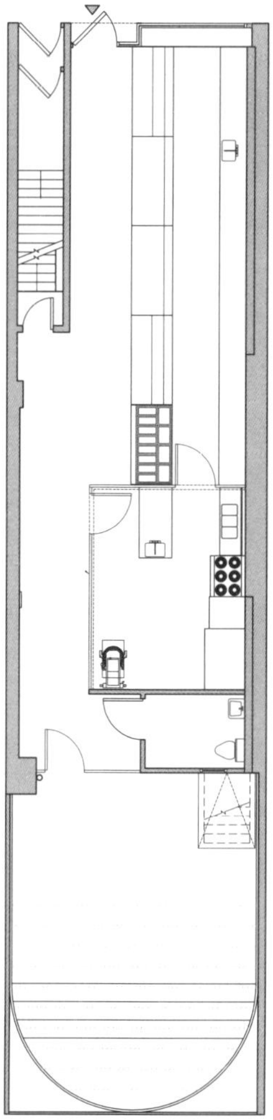

Floor plan

Cheerful atmosphere created by bright colors

- **Project name**
  Padarie
- **Location**
  Porto Alegre, Brazil
- **Site area**
  2691 square feet
  (250 square meters)
- **Completion**
  2013
- **Interior design**
  MAG arquiteturas
- **Photography**
  Marcelo Donadussi

Established in a two-story building, this project started with three main guidelines: order, zoning, and intelligent flows. The ground floor houses the customer area and some of the support facilities: the tearoom, the store, the cashier, the counter, the restrooms, a small backyard, the storage room, a small kitchen, and the locker rooms and bathrooms for the staff. At the top floor, the designers found the administration office, another storage room, the bakery, the patisserie, and the cold chamber.

The original staircase was relocated to make circulation more efficient and dynamic. The service areas are all connected. The counter and the display for the breads were designed to make good use of the room below the stairs.

The tables, chairs and benches at the customer area were all painted in different bright colors, bringing a sense of lightness to the room. At the back, the little store and the cashier are located near the stylized saloon door that leads to the restrooms. It's

all very clean, yet full of inspired details. At some parts of the walls, the painting is a little worn, revealing the solid brick layer that lies underneath. The pillars are covered with pinus elliotti. The lighting completes the ambience, with articulated luminaries and rail spotlights. To add character and personality, the cashier and the counter were coated with rectangular white tiles.

A special mask was applied to the existing façade to provide privacy to the storage room and the office without blocking the sunlight. This solution was accomplished with a set of colored metal brises shaped like the wheat spike, the main ingredient of the bread. A wooden pergola completes the façade, limiting the outdoor sitting area. The elements of this project were designed to grant personality and a strong identity to the first Padarie shop in town.

Elevations

Sections

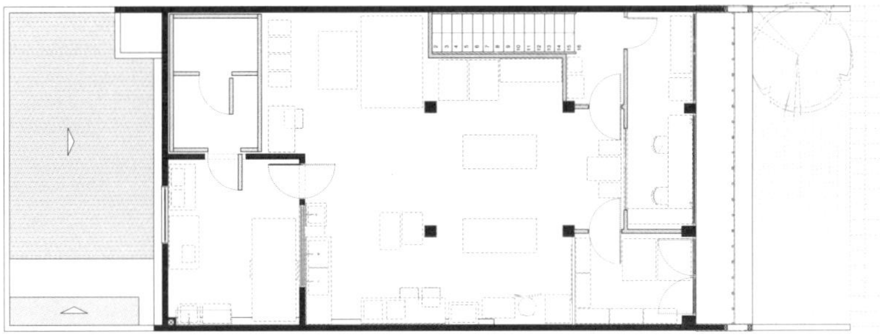

Second-floor plan

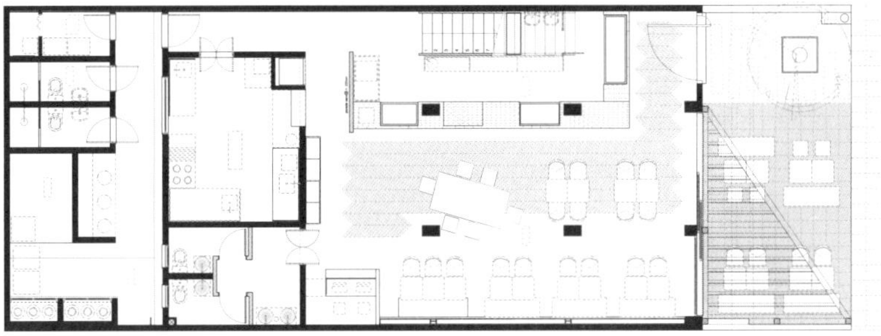

First-floor plan

Mix-and-match design of nature and industrial style

- **Project name**
  Panemar Polus Center Bakery
- **Location**
  Cluj-Napoca, Transylvania, Romania
- **Site area**
  1507 square feet (140 square meters)
- **Completion**
  2018
- **Interior design**
  Todor Cosmin Studio
- **Photography**
  Em Iova

This store is part of the Panemar bakery chain in Cluj-Napoca (Transylvania, Romania), the idea behind the creative concept being the reinterpretation and revival of traditional values in a contemporary manner. The design sought to reveal brand values of passion and confidence while also to encompassing the essence of the products, which is freshness, naturalness, and simplicity.

The furniture, the floor, the decorative rustic timber, and the volumetric logo found on one of the lateral walls are all made of natural, rough-hewn wood, resembling the color of wheat. The central element is the countertop—a combination of wood and glass cubes appearing to be suspended above a pattern made out of ceramic pieces. The fresh feeling drifts from the shades of green in the upholstery that covers the chairs, armchairs, and sofas; other materials like metal, wood, ceramics, glass, and natural stone are harmoniously combined and give great dynamic to the interior of the bakery.

At the same time, the large windows bordering the space on two sides and all the elements made in glass offer an altogether perfect transparency to the space, ensuring a better visual connection between the interior and the exterior; between the bakery and the commercial gallery hosting it. The combination of natural and fresh blends in contrast with the industrial style of the ceiling on which the electrical wiring remains visible. The brick walls and large windows with a metal frame give a loft-style appearance, everything blending perfectly to create a warm, simple, and welcoming feeling.

The initial challenge to finding a mix between the old and new, traditional and contemporary was overcome to create an animated and attractive space for social interaction, which was one of the biggest purposes for the designers.

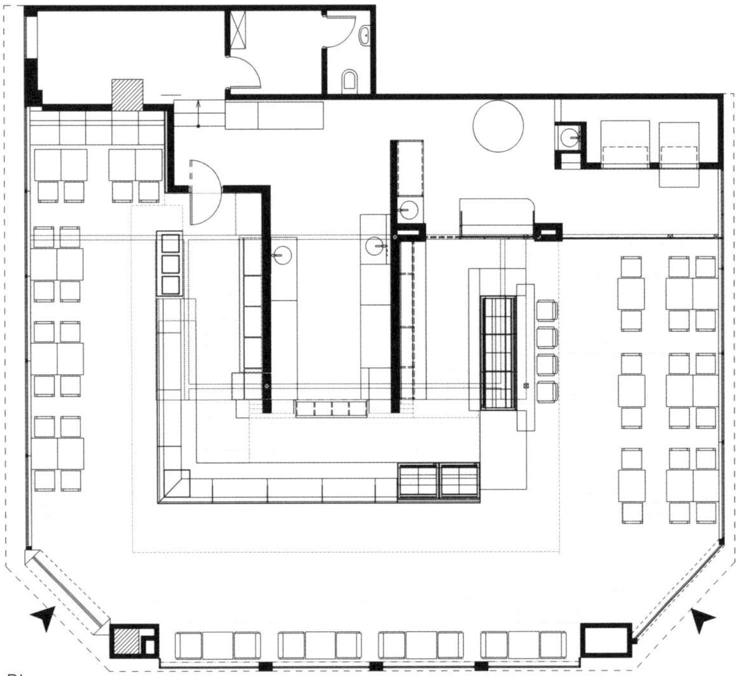

Plan

cadoro mobili

Delicate space presented by “softwalls” and warm-white light

- **Project name**
  Pâtisserie Petit Lapin
- **Location**
  Westmount, Canada
- **Site area**
  3681 square feet
  (342 square meters)
- **Completion**
  2015
- **Interior design**
  Architecture Open Form
- **Photography**
  Adrien Williams

Situated on Victoria Avenue in Westmount, the Pâtisserie Petit Lapin occupies a small commercial space of 3681 square feet (342 square meters) in a basement with a 6-foot-wide (180-centimeter-wide) hall connecting it to its street-level entrance. The challenge was to peak the curiosity of passersby in order to lure them inside. To do this, MXMA Architecture & Design, led by architect Maxime Moreau, created a series of textured surfaces, with a modular system of “softwalls” with integrated LED lights, to present the pastries, highlight the double-height entrance hall, and give the space an illusion of grandeur. The softwalls unfold in a continuous gesture on the walls and various ceilings, leading customers in the transition between the retail entry and the downstairs counter.

The pastry shop is minimalist in décor and very bright in order to showcase the customized creations of the pastry chef and to create a visual focus that is visible from the street both during the day and at night. Suspended like a continuous work of art

along the walls and ceilings between the street level and the basement, the flexible LED strips, which emit a warm white hue, were integrated into the modular system of the softwalls; this amazing source of light highlights the delicacy of the white textile fiber modules and renders the expression of their fluid motion even more magical. The pastries come to life as the light travels within the lines and folds of the translucent fibers.

The visual identity of the pastry shop is defined not only by its delicate and velvety pastel shades, but even more so by its textures and its continuous surfaces. The flexible softwalls partition system symbolizes the undulations and flexibility of the parchment paper liners used for baking cupcakes. The translucent white modules, made of 100 percent recyclable polyethylene, help sculpt the light and reveal the delicate structure of the folds. The softwalls and the white quartz countertops move from the street-level entry into the basement shop, creating a homogeneous project that expresses the link between identity and structure and underlining the concept of continuity in motion through orderly spatial organization and the alignment of objects, desserts, and spaces.

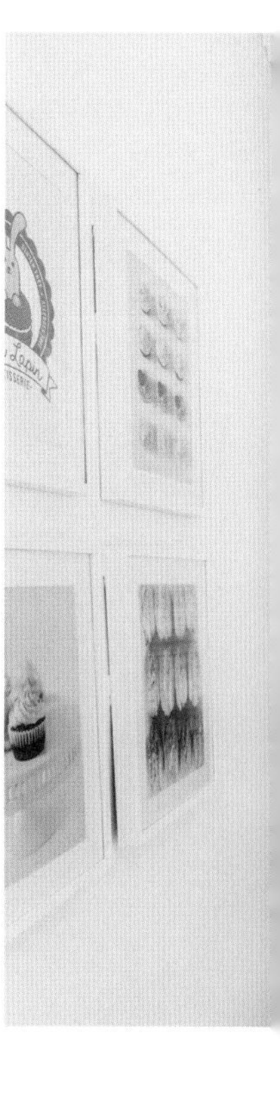

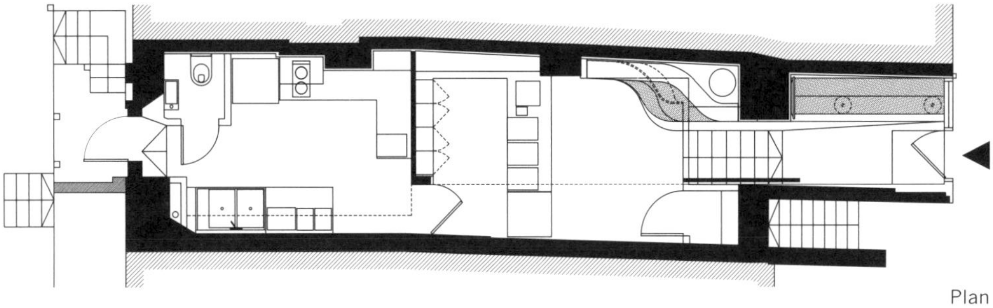

Plan

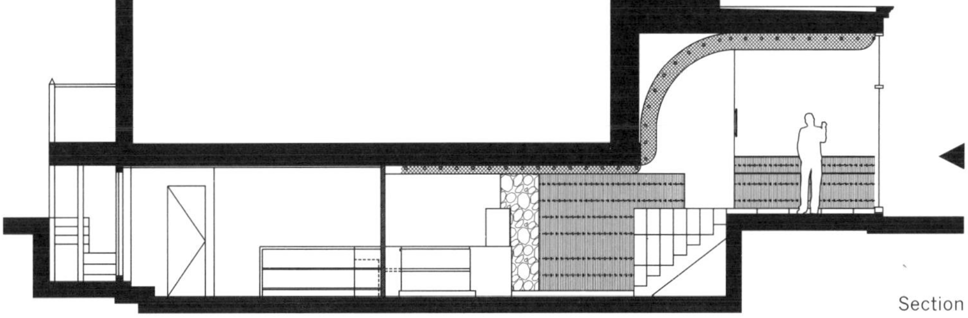

Section

Rotation space shuttling between green leaves and twigs

- **Project name**
  TiensTiens Café
- **Location**
  Sanlitun, Beijing, China
- **Site area**
  1464 square feet
  (136 square meters)
- **Completion**
  2015
- **Architectural design**
  TAO (Trace Architecture Office)
- **Photography**
  Chen Hao

Located in Beijing Mechanotronics Compound, inside Sanlitun district—which is one of the upscale neighborhoods in Beijing between Sanlitun SOHO to the west side of the site and Sanlitun Village to the northwest—TiensTiens is a French dessert shop, the roof of which and surrounding buildings are used as a bar at night.

Within the 640-square-foot (59.5-square-meter) site, one of the special features in the design process was the two poplars inside with strong trunks and diameters of around 18 inches (45 centimeters). One of the two trees has a big branch separate from the main trunk at the level of 8.2 feet (2.5 meters), while more than 10 additional poplars are scatter around. The client also rented the rooftop of the HK restaurant neighboring to use as an outdoor terrace, which is 2034 square feet (189 square meters) and has six poplars sticking out of the roof.

As a dessert shop, the first level has the functions of showing, selling, and the

kitchen itself. The upper floors are dining areas and the rooftop is outdoor space that can be used as dining space or a terrace.

The main question of this design was how to draw customers in to experience the space. As a solution, the design separates the second floor into three different heights. By using light steel structures and a big area of translucent glass, these small platforms seem to be floating in the air and make it very easy for customers to feel the spirally space sequence. In this way, the design provides various kinds of contact among people, as well as between people and the trees.

The building was split into platforms of different heights due of the two big trees. The spaces of different scales provide people with various kinds of contact with the trees. The stairs spiral up between the leaves and branches.

Perspective

Sections

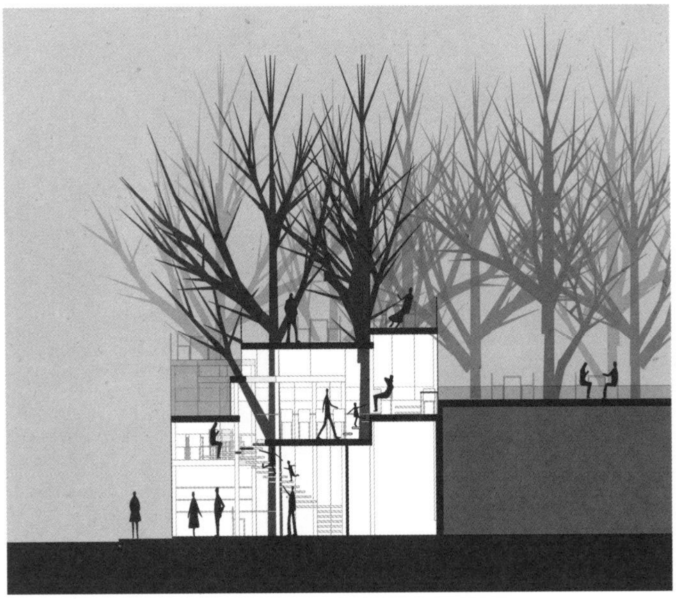

Simplified Japanese style in light-gray

- **Project name**
  Style Bakery
- **Location**
  Kiryu, Gunma, Japan
- **Site area**
  3014 square feet
  (280 square meters)
- **Completion**
  2013
- **Interior design**
  SNARK
- **Photography**
  Ippei Shinzawa

In Kiryu, Gunma, Japan, Style Bakery was opened as the first prototype shop with a future view of store development. Renovating the long-established bakery operating since 1930, the shop aimed to be a new type of enterprise, incorporating the features of both locally owned and globally franchised stores.

A light gray, which is the concept color of the brand, was used in tiles, lights, steel frames, and a dirt floor. Variations of materials used balance the color tint within the space, bringing out the interior of the patisserie. Solid oaks were used for the top panel so as to enhance the warmth of the bread. Maximizing the height and the width of the windows and selecting a slim frame, it brings brightness and freshness to the room.

Fluorescent lamps were embedded into the ceiling, which makes the space look clean. Larger furniture in the center and the spot shade above the cashier build vertical height internally. Created line of flows, with the simplified designs and arrangements of

furniture and lined LED lights equipped down under the parietal shelves, enable the customers to select and carry their baked goods in comfort.

The space right next to the shelf is refrigerated so that foods like sandwiches can be displayed. The eat-in counter, located next to the cashier, was made with the same solid oak as the top panel, and uses the marine lamps. The logo decorated on the wall beside the cashier was made from steel plates.

The signboard, which represents the shop, is a neon lamp, and the entrance and exit signs are located on both sides. Additional attention was paid to the needs of children and the elderly to secure their paths, by sloping the way from the parking area.

Using light gray as the concept color of the brand, the shop holds a sense of unity, and a bright and clean atmosphere at the same time, together with woods, soft lightning, and natural sunlight from the windows.

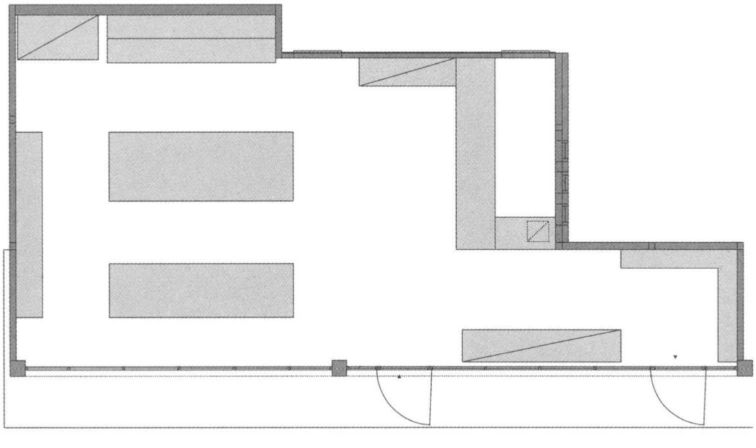

Plan

The warmth under the clusters of lighting

- **Project name**
  Ströck Feierabend
- **Location**
  Vienna, Austria
- **Site area**
  1324 square feet
  (123 square meters)
- **Completion**
  2014
- **Interior design**
  JHP Design
- **Photography**
  Ströck

Viennese bakery chain Ströck launched a new store, Ströck Feierabend, a dine-in bakery and wine bar hybrid in Vienna. The design consultancy had been working with Ströck since 2012, and the latest store format was developed by JHP in response to Ströck acquiring an adjoining site to one of its current bakeries and the desire to trade beyond the hours within which a typical bakery would operate.

Ströck Feierabend was born: an innovative concept that functions as a fully operational bakery during the day and as a restaurant and wine bar at night, all built around the chain's core product—bread.

To benefit from the longer trading hours, Ströck developed a new menu, serving up its range all based around bread paired with ideal accompaniments such as soup, cut meats, salad, as well evening favorites such as pizza. The new store operates a dine-in and takeaway service, and compliments Ströck's bakery range with only the finest Viennese coffee, local beers, and Austrian wine.

The store concept was industrial and utilitarian in its roots, employing a simple textured range of materials and finishes such as bar counter tops made from copper, bleached timber on the bar-front, stone-clad walls, and warm tone tiles specially laid in a herringbone formation.

The key features of the new venue are the extremely long bar, which runs from the bakery to the bistro, the back wall of which is designed to be an ever-changing blackboard, and the 80 suspended glass jar light fittings, which captivate those walking past at night time. For the store's opening, its owners commissioned local artists known to the Ströck family to create illustrations for the blackboard wall.

The store's façade was reconfigured to unify both neighboring stores, and its cement rendered front and industrial-style metal frames exuding the essence of a classic urban bakery. JHP worked on all aspects of the new store's architecture, retail design, visual merchandising, product display and food presentation, brand communication, menus, and uniforms. The core success of the project was from the creative working partnership of Ströck Managing Director Christoph Ströck and JHP Managing Director Raj Wilkinson.

BROT IST
UNSER LEBEN,
SO EINFACH
IST DAS ...
SCHON GEW
→ 100% österreichi
→ Handwerkliches
→ Rezepte ohne Zu
bei allen Brot- &
Kleingebäcksorten
Brot & Wein

Plan

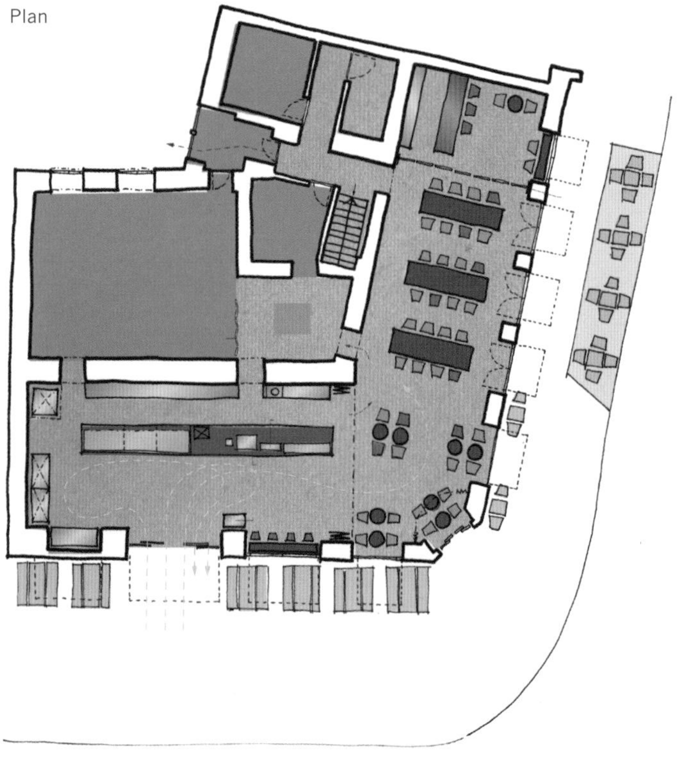

Feierabend
Brot & Wein
EST. 2013
→ 100% österreichi
→ Handwerkliches
→ Rezepte ohne Zus
bei allen Brot- &
Kleingebäcksorten

The sweetness of sugar crystal

- **Project name**
  Shugaa
- **Location**
  Bangkok, Thailand
- **Site area**
  1076 square feet
  (100 square meters)
- **Completion**
  2016
- **Interior design**
  party/space/design
- **Photography**
  F Sections

Shugaa is a French-style dessert bar located in Ekamai offering delicate sweets by a Thai chef, who designed a creative menu and desserts that always surprise and amaze the customers. These dessert menus became the inspiration for the interior design of Shugaa, which display sugar elements everywhere throughout.

The concept of the interior design of Shugaa was researched from the idea of the molecules and crystals of sugar itself. Seen from the outside through the glass wall, a hanging polygon installation reminiscent of sugar crystals can be seen by passersby. Timber was also used in the design, together with a mint-green color, to create a warm and earthy atmosphere. The design team added a dash of modern luxury by using tones of rose gold and a marble counter.

The first zone of the dessert room is for customers to sit and enjoy their food. Sitting at the bar, customers can see the polygon-shaped wall, which was made from

a special building technique and creates an interesting dimension to the room. A rose-gold lighting installation was hung along the ceiling wall, and the first zone was connected to the upstairs zone by a spiral staircase, which is the focal point of the room. The magic of design created this "sugar crystal" staircase using acrylic boxes arranged along the curve of the spiral staircase, which is iconic of the Shugaa dessert bar.

When customers walk to the second floor, they are greeted by a view of the dessert preparation by the chef. Further beyond is a private area that is ideal for quite relaxing while enjoying a dessert, reading or working.

It can also be rearranged as a workshop area open for dessert and fondant making for those with a passion for making their own desserts.

SHUGAA
room for dessert

SHUGAA
room for dessert

First-floor plan

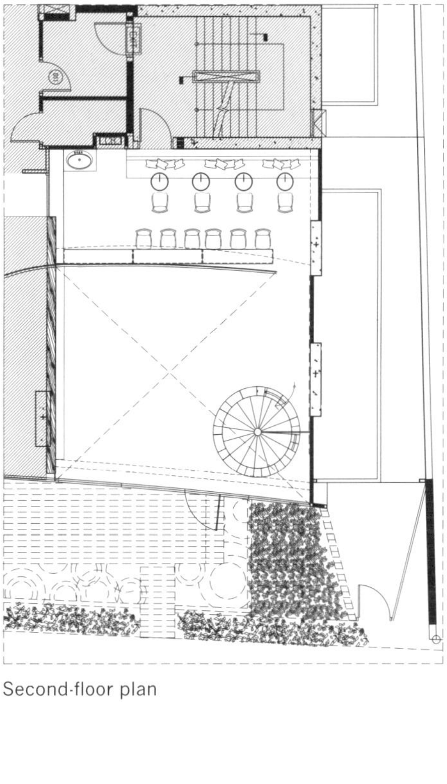

Second-floor plan

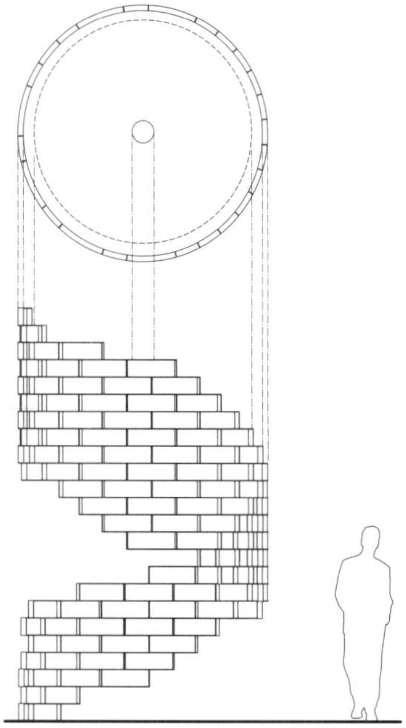

Front view of stair

Stair perspective 1

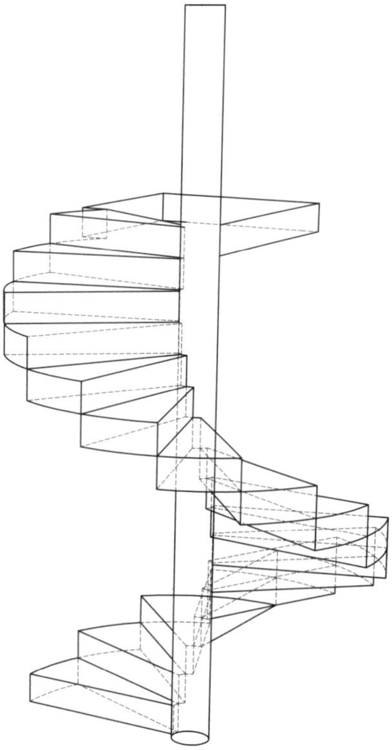

Stair perspective 2

Open space with fashion and simplicity

- **Project name**
  Savoidakis Bakery & Patisserie
- **Location**
  Rethymno Crete, Greece
- **Site area**
  6458 square feet (600 square meters)
- **Completion**
  2017
- **Interior design**
  Manousos Leontarakis & Associates
- **Photography**
  Yiannis Fais

This project involved the full renovation of Savoidakis Bakery & Patisserie in Rethymno Crete by Manousos Leontarakis & Associates.

The 1968-square-foot (600-square-meter) building, which houses the Savoidakis bakery & patisserie, was demolished and redesigned from scratch, putting the emphasis inside the store and in the design of the display cases to offer the best product presentation. The baked goods in the display cabinet are arranged in an orderly manner to look neat and appetizing. Branching off the bakery, there are many outdoor dining areas where customers can enjoy food and watch the scenery along the way. The building design used a lot of large glass walls, making the store look bright and clean. At the same time, the indoor and outdoor environments were well integrated.

The materials used in the display cases were glass, marble, and wood. Generally, these materials are prevalent in the space. For the lighting, the designers used hanging

luminaries, which were designed by the office team with LED lighting. The lighting also plays a very good decorative role.

The earthy colors chosen create a very warm atmosphere inside in harmony with the materials used in the display cases and the brick wall. The shop's workshops were designed to be visible from the space where the client interacts. The colors used in the store design are more harmonious. Floors, walls, display cabinets are very close in colors. There is a comic on the wall, which is related to the baking process. It not only serves as a decoration in the room, but also fits well with the theme of the bakery.

Outside the shop a coffee room was created where metal tables and chairs were combined to fit perfectly with the style chosen inside the bakery.

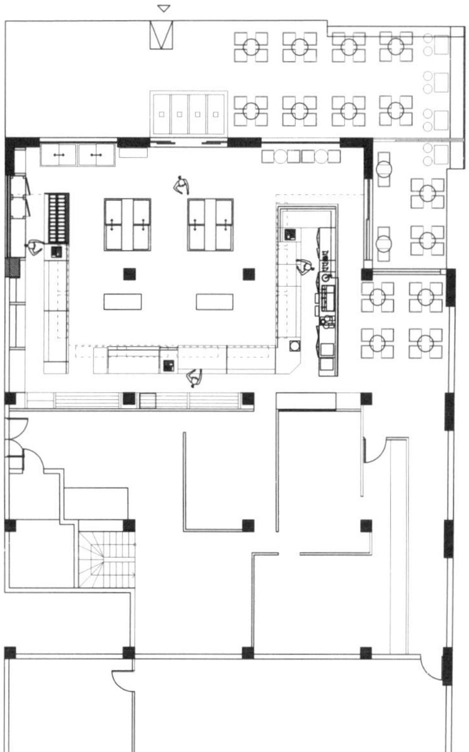

Plan

Open space of traditions and nature

- **Project name**
  Der Bäcker Ruetz
- **Location**
  Kematen, Austria
- **Site area**
  2691 square feet
  (250 square meters)
- **Completion**
  2011
- **Interior design**
  JHP Design
- **Photography**
  Sarah Collis

Austrian bakery client Der Bäcker Ruetz opened a flagship store in the Austrian town of Kematen. The store was created to be a destination for all things bakery with an open-plan production area and kitchens, café, retail space, private dining areas, a lecture hall, a museum showcasing the history of baking, and a children's play area. Deeply rooted in the bakery chain's values are those of authenticity, tradition, innovation, and community—all of which are found in the experience in-store.

JHP's work includes consideration of the strategic positioning, architectural alteration and treatments, planning and layout, the entire retail environment and experience, name generation, identity, and communication. The challenge for JHP was to incorporate the origins of bread and the baking process into the store. The environmental backdrop to the store uses a palette of materials inherent in baking—rich timber, baked clay, and the color-ways of the brand reflect its key product. Along with the bakery paddles that adorn the

walls, LCD screens were also installed showing slow-moving images of cascading water, barley swaying in a gentle breeze, and furnace fires, further reinforcing the “rustica modern” approach to the store design. The aroma from the baking process is pumped around the store area to stimulate and attract customers who can eat in-store in a café area, or take food home.

Throughout the store, the bread-making process is clearly visible and the expression of “abundance” is fundamental. From the merchandising of the produce through to the graphic communication of its ingredients, customers are left in no doubt as to Ruetz’s offer—selling wholesome breads, baked naturally using traditional ingredients. The retailer has a keen focus on health, organizing their own half marathon, and bringing entertainment to the store in the form of kids’ baking days.

Steve Collis, JHP joint Managing Director, commented, “Ruetz is just the type of client the designers love to work with—heaving with initiatives, powerful brand heritage, and is absolutely passionate about its products and customer service. The new store design and corporate identity will galvanize their brand proposition.” JHP developed the brand platform,

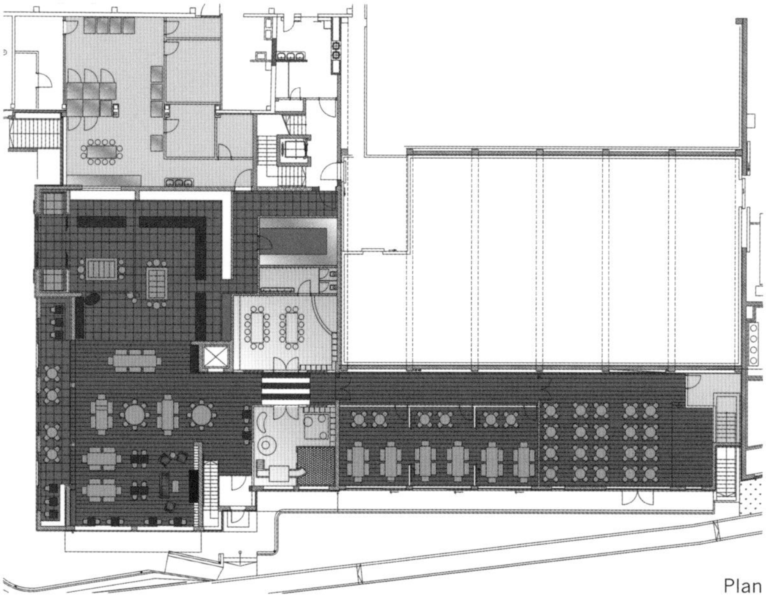

Plan

communication pathway, in-store communications, service strategy, packaging, and uniforms, as well as the store design. Since then Ruetz, the viennoiserie, bakery of astonishing cakes and coffees have opened a number of bakery outlets where JHP Design have been involved with developing the brand identity and strategically leading the way in which they visually display their products.

Der
Bäcker
Ruetz

Der
Bäcker
Ruetz

Heartwarming atmosphere from the oak logs

- **Project name**
  Pinocchio
- **Location**
  Yokohama, Kanagawa, Japan
- **Site area**
  506 square feet (47 square meters)
- **Completion**
  2016
- **Interior design**
  I IN
- **Photography**
  Satoshi Shigeta (I IN)

Opening its doors to customers in 2016, a unique bakery located at the landmark Matsubara shopping street in Japan's Yokohama city, Kanagawa prefecture created a unique new place in the busy neighborhood for its clients to experience freshly-baked bread and pastries called Pinocchio.

The wide street-facing façade is visible directly from the road, catching the eye of customers with its soft façade lighting, which further emphasizes the flow of the seasons and the shift of day into night. The bakery logo was also specifically designed for the store with a minimal approach, allowing it to be visible from a distance, yet not distracting the open façade view.

Upon entering the store, customers are immediately attracted to the core of the space. A solid wooden table, installed at the center of the store, dominates the space to create an immediate and unforgettable impression. On the long recycled oak surface sit straw baskets and trays filled

with walnut loaves, buttery croissants, savory focaccias, and nightingale bean breads, baked by Chef Masahito Kanou. The industrial lighting over the counter creates an impressive theatrical spotlight—a strong focus point that presents the bread and pastries in an intuitively natural setting.

The unique irregularity and texture of the wood, achieved over time, creates a high-quality expression to the space. By installing a long table in the middle of the bakery, the design studio achieved in

creating a simultaneously external and internal form that is easily visible and recognizable from the street. After several visits to the timber factory, while selecting most suitable wood, the designers finally encountered the perfect 9.8-foot (3-meter) long oak log, also called "kashi" in Japanese. The connection between the ideal material, the designers, and the client was instant. The oak will naturally expand with time and use, therefore a steel plate was inserted into its core to prevent it from bolstering and cracking, and it was finished with an oil coating, preserving its natural look and qualities. The log became the central piece of Pinocchio.

Cool mortar surrounds the rest of the space, creating a contrast between the natural materials and allowing a neutral environment for the delicious-looking baked goods. The rest of the display on the wall was created by a minimal eyeline shelves, allowing the baked products to stand out. A warm-hued woven rug generates a home-like atmosphere.

The biggest challenge in the project and for the designers was creating a strong impression with minimal elements, allowing a heartwarming environment for the store and its clients, leaving the experience of the neighborhood town bakery to charm with its fresh-baked goods.

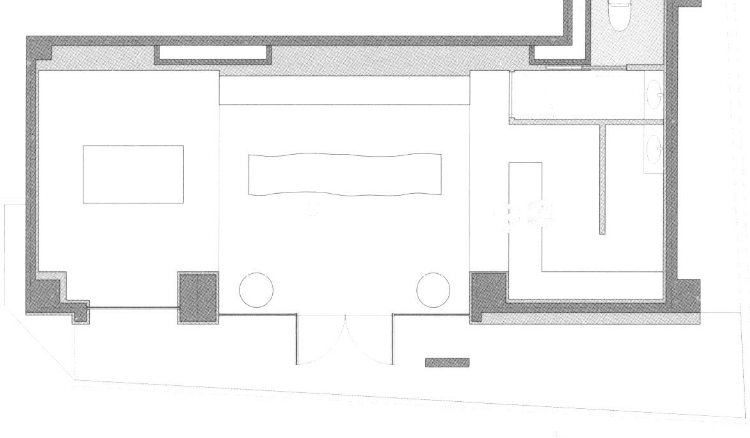

Plan

Experiencing space combined with actual and visual scenes

- **Project name**
  A Breathing Cake Shop—MarierWagashi
- **Location**
  Shenzhen, China
- **Site area**
  1259 square feet (117 square meters)
- **Completion**
  2017
- **Interior design**
  BloomDesign
- **Photography**
  Nie Xiaocong

"Marier" in Japanese means intimacy or intimate connection between people. MarierWagashi's first heritage shop is situated in Shangmeilin, Shenzhen, on the ground floor of an old building in an old community that has an air of detachment from the urban hustle.

For Li Baolong and Chen Xiaohu from BloomDesign, each project has a story, and this cake shop was no different, where the hero is 64-years-old Maruyama, founder of the Marier brand, whose lifelong pursuit of creating the best cakes manifests the professional spirit of striving for perfection. The designers needed to tell this story through the language of design.

BloomDesign inherited the simple philosophy of "selecting natural ingredients to make the best cake" that the Marier brand has insisted on for over 40 years. They stove to keep the design minimalist while focusing on natural materials to embellish the large space, thus illustrating the simple and reserved qualities of Marier brand.

Inside the space, the materials pursue an authentic and pure beauty with raw stone, unprocessed timber, and terrazzo flooring, which work to abandon an overly decorative or foppish appearance. An old tree outside the window interacts with a huge original rock inside the shop through a narrow glass curtain wall, drawing nature into the environment to immerse the clients in its calming presence. While enjoying a cup of Taiwanese cold-brewing tea paired with Japanese wagashi, leisurely afternoon tea time becomes textured and organic.

All of the design solutions follow the Marier brand's idea of natural health, from the earth-like color and natural texture to the unadorned furnishings and natural ornament. Through minimalistic visual language and design techniques, BloomDesign created a multi-level artistic conception of "seeing a mountain in a rock and a forest in a tree" that is typical in the Eastern context. Clients can enjoy a natural environment away from the bustling city.

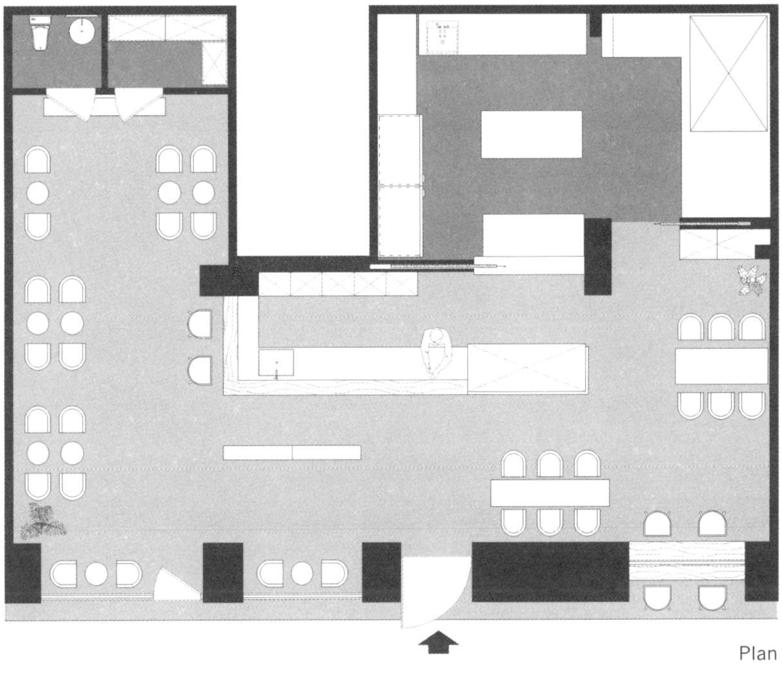

Plan

Gray space filled with scientific and technological senses

- **Project name**
  Booth's Cake
- **Location**
  Beijing, China
- **Site area**
  5157 square feet
  (480 square meters)
- **Completion**
  2016
- **Interior design**
  odd
- **Photography**
  Ruijing Photography

Okamoto Deguchi Design was invited by Booth's Cake to design their new store at Gongti North Road in Beijing. The client wanted a new space that would give customers a unique visual feeling and a comfortable dining experience.

Walking along the noisy Gongti North Road, the building stands out with its rough grey walls and a grass-green logo surrounded by local residential buildings. It is simple and modern, yet integrated.

The space is divided into two floors. On the first floor are the display counter and the kitchen. Full-height glass walls attract passing customers into the store to look around. Gentle grey tones, sloped walls, a stainless-steel walkway, and seating furniture areas matching the décor highlight the space's clean and futuristic style. The 29.5-foot (9-meter) display counter forms a centralized display. The clear lines and simple décor give sharp contrast with the exquisite handmade cakes, emphasizing the softness and delicate sensitivity of the cakes.

The second floor focuses on the guests' dining experience, using wood to give a warm balance to the grey tones. The stainless-steel walkway connects the whole space, allowing the three spaces to feel connected while maintaining their own unique characteristics. Each area has well-designed elements, such as the windows-embedded sofa seats and the long table, which could be used for pastry classes. In addition, the original low beam was designed for the logo wall. The combination of simple materials and lighting also enriches the whole space.

BOOTH'S CAKE
THE REAL TASTE YOU NEED
BOOTH'S CAKE

BOOTH'S CAKE

Second-floor plan

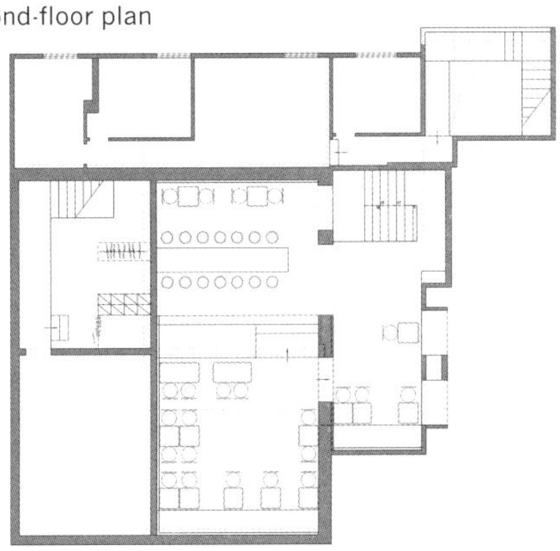

First-floor plan

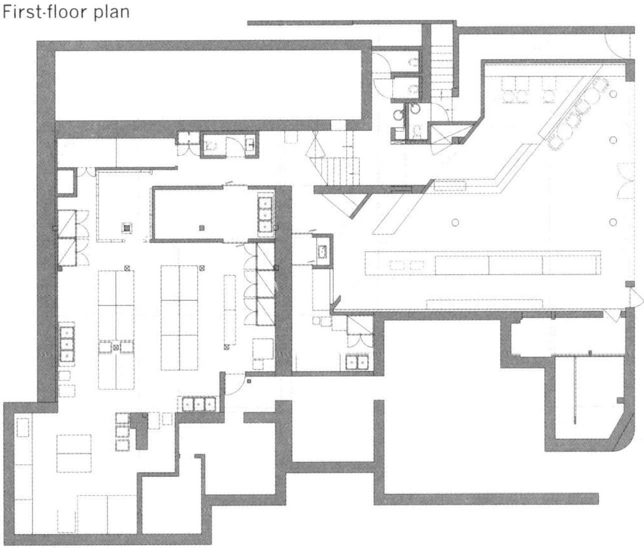

All-white space dominated by a long specular cabinet

- **Project name**
  Des Choux et Des Idees
- **Location**
  Abd el Wahhab El Inglizi, Achrafieh, Beirut, Lebanon
- **Site area**
  215 square feet
  (20 square meters)
- **Completion**
  2017
- **Interior design**
  Studio Etienne Bastormagi
- **Photography**
  Wissam Chaaya

Located in a prime neighborhood in Beirut, a parking spot for a residential building was converted into a pastry shop. Designed by Studio Etienne Bas, the 215-square-foot (20-square-meter) contemporary shop is the flagship store for the brand Des Choux et Des Idees.

Integrating the retail and the street experience, the architect used an "urban mirror" to reflect the pastries for passersby. Over the course of the day, the urban mirror gradually changes its positioning with a manual process reflecting passersby instead of merchandise. The different reflections based on opening hours aim at extending the street into the store and vice versa.

The store, a monochromatic space, brings together mainly different white textures and materials. The all-white feeling of the store showcases the pastries, which become the jewels highlighted within the space, reminiscent to an art collection in a white cube museum. The latter concept reflects the layering of pastries served by the store.

Axonometric

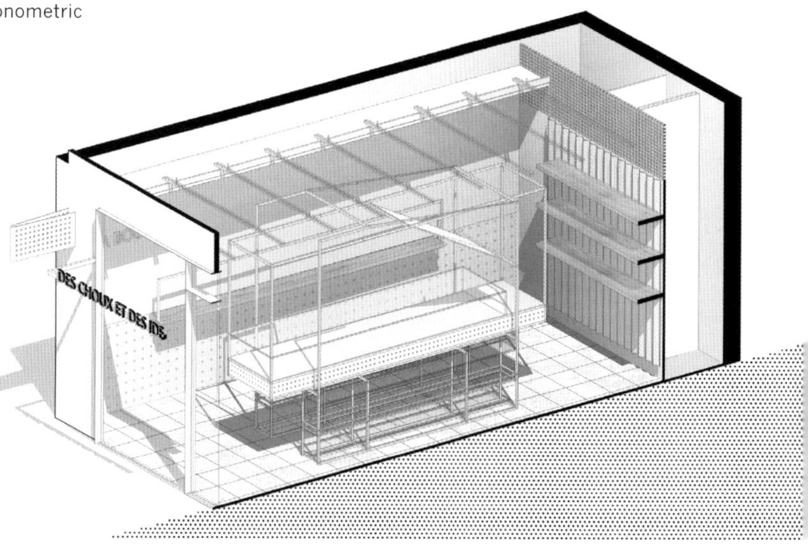

The shop's layout concentrates on the previous use of the store, where a central machine was the basis of the dimensions of the space created to inhabit it. The new shop embraces a new structure that becomes an integral part of the boutiques' design.

The circulation in the shop revolves around a central structure that inhabits the main display fridge, the cashier, a storage space, the urban mirror as well as indirect lighting for the unit. The structure is entirely composed of a 0.8-inch (2-centimeter) steel structure white painted profile like a wireframe.

The materials used in the shop were locally produced and fabricated—from the steel to the wood type to the mirror and the paint as well as the textured patterns—part of a sustainable approach in the design principle.

The studio's design focuses on developing an experience out of the retail of Des Choux Et Des Idees, creating a new design challenge for the brand.

European-style space comprising velvet, and blue wood

- **Project name**
  Gaudenti 1971 Po
- **Location**
  Turin, Italy
- **Site area**
  1550 square feet
  (144 square meters)
- **Completion**
  2018
- **Interior design**
  lamatilde
- **Photography**
  PEPEfotografia

The design of Gaudenti 1971 Po mixed the format of the small, Italian fine pastry shop with a large international bakery. This was the starting point to define a space that could convey both respect for the traditional values of Italian confectionery culture and a strong drive for renewal. This premise translated into a careful renovation of existing elements, which were systematically integrated into the new décor. While a different graphic motif was designed for each venue, giving a new interpretation of historical decorative styles, the consistent use of velvet and blue wood ensures the brand is instantly recognizable.

Gaudenti's third venue is located in a 19th-century historic building of Via Po, one of most iconic streets of Turin city center, inside a former leather-goods factory.

The original wood paneling from the early 1950s was renovated to lighten up the overall décor and make it more delicate. In the same way, the ceiling coffers were altered and used for the new LED lighting

system that gives the store an evocative luminous grid. Furthermore, blades of light echo the same geometric pattern introduced in the Carlo Felice location, the second venue opened by the company. The theatrical staircase that connects the two floors was freed and turned into part of the sitting area. As the space was much more narrow, the windows were turned into little décor sitting areas, just like in the first Gaudenti. In addition, the use of mirrors allowed enlarging of the perception of space, while the two Empire-style twin chandeliers increased the emphasis on the décor.

The original hardwood floors had been gravely damaged by previous carpeting, but were recovered almost entirely. When restoration was not possible, they were replaced with resin flooring that clearly declares with its contrast a new solution, instead of hiding it.

Finally, Gaudenti 1971 Po presents more baroque influences, if not Rococo: a gentler Baroque, typical of Turin.

Plan

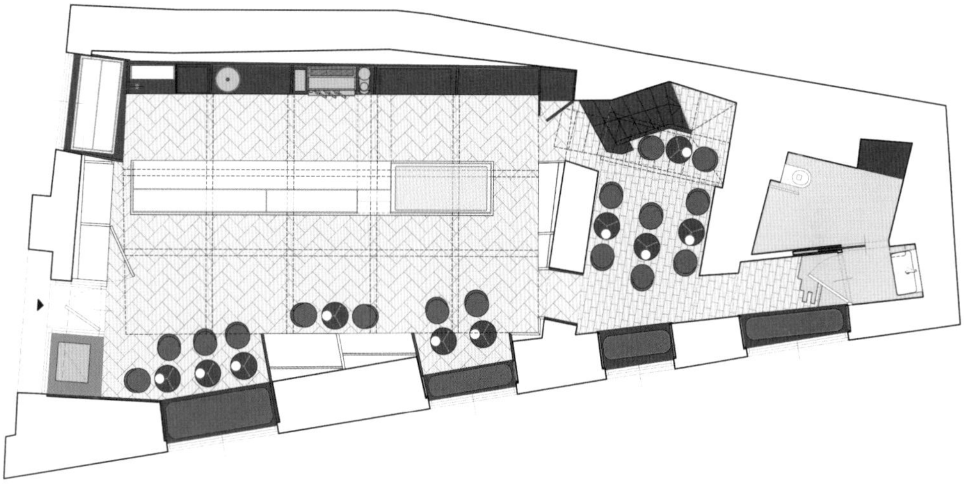

Section

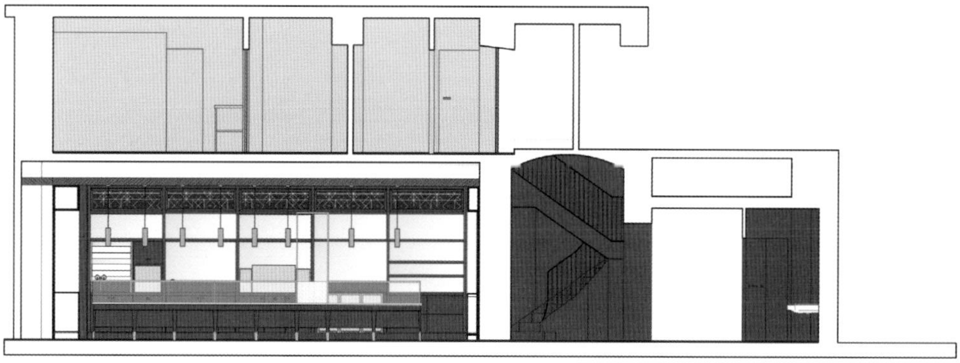

Restructured space with square log shelves

- **Project name**
  Beauty Free Baking
- **Location**
  Wuhan, China
- **Site area**
  2207 square feet
  (205 square meters)
- **Completion**
  2016
- **Interior design**
  Zones design Studio
- **Photography**
  Xia Xuwei

The project was located in the Han Street, Wuchang District, Wuhan City, near the Wanda Plaza, covering an area of 2207 square feet (205 square meters) with two floors, with the aim of providing customers with a satisfying service and dining environment.

Timber, square white tiles, and pendant lighting create a comfortable and leisurely environment for the space. The main concept of interior design lies in the spatial restructuring, which was displayed by distinctive wooden ceiling shelves as if they are traveling through the store as blocks of color. The off-white tiling extends along the wall surface, forming a façade space. With the soft outdoor light created by the characteristic chandelier decorated by the ball-type bulbs, the lighting offers an atmosphere of Western restaurants. The outdoor greenery is drawn in through the windows into the interior space, integrating into a wonderful spatial experience.

The interior style is based on the loft design, and a large amount of timber beams and

steel mesh were used in construction. The gray and white emulsion paints were used as the background wall, so as to set off the texture of the beams.

The dining hall, on the one hand, uses the simple industrial metal material and pinewood square shelves extending from the ground to the top surface, and on the other hand, applies the bright white square bricks and glasses to the cook's workbench and the selling window, both of which are in sharp contrast. The crisscrossed wooden shelves and black steel play a certain role in blocking and dividing space. Industrial elements and soft baking ornaments are largely used in space accessories, and the matching of the black steel structure and wooden structure not only delineates the form of each space, but also create a unique human flow line in the restaurant. Stairs were made of transverse battens and vertical hang springs, forming a crisscrossed space, and the decoration of a rolling pin make the space more unique.

On the second floor, in the dining area, the designer used soft blue bench seats to quieten the interior space, where customers could enjoy a delicious meal at ease. The hanging timber grille and the black chandelier were combined into the central area of the hall, and the black ceiling naturally integrates into the background, so as to highlight the unity of the main space. The atmosphere is dominated by gray. The black, white, and grey bricks were matched with the cement-colored wall and the soft light outside the windows, forming an atmospheric space with the hanging spring and the rolling pins sending out a unique texture under the reflection of backlight.

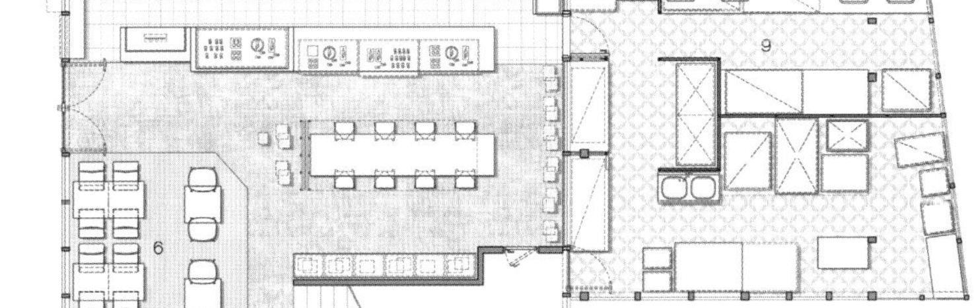

First-floor plan

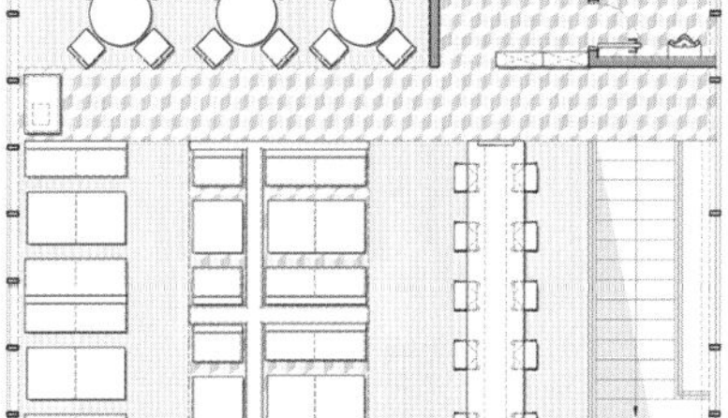

Second-floor plan

Glass house within a house full of hierarchy sense

- **Project name**
  Home Bakery
- **Location**
  Taipei, Taiwan, China
- **Site area**
  237 square feet
  (22 square meters)
- **Completion**
  2017
- **Interior design**
  Fullhouse (Joy Chen)
- **Photography**
  Hey! Cheese Photography

Situated in a quiet and leisurely locale, the bakery is positioned on a ground-floor storefront facing the street, with large-area windows, which are quite rare in the metropolitan areas. Although the actual area is only about 237 square feet (22 square meters), the interior is about 13 feet (4 meters) high, with a foursquare pattern and excellent lighting.

After the designer made repeated inspections, he gutted the interior and crafted a new artsy style, fusing the light French elements and American living sentiment in order to create a functional space that met the requirements of the design brief.

Passersby are attracted to the space, which comprises a large round window, French carved pillars, and beautiful light and shadow, drawing in curious visitors. The space was deliberately arranged to include the entrance at the center of building, the two symmetrical shop windows on both sides, the display surface, and even the visitors' moving line and sight line.

Upon entering, the L-shaped kitchen island facing the doorway is the first sight greeting the customers, with the white cabinet with a deep-wood-colored tabletop displaying the various specialty pastries, which are perfectly displayed to make customers' mouths water. Another blue-glass bench is decorated with a specially convex white porcelain water tank, tiles on the tabletop, and white relief bricks on the wall and wall-mounted titanium-plated holders.

As a professional bakery, the kitchen is absolutely critical, but due to the size restrictions of the space, the designer made good use of the interior height, with iron framework plus four kinds of clear glass and retro flower glass, creating a glass box as a house within a house behind the kitchen island, the oblique eave of which shows the three-dimensional beauty of the structure. The hazy lighting and shadow, set off by the flower glass, conveniently modifies the cluttered scene in the kitchen.

In order to create a casual home-style feeling without losing the tonality of texture, the designer listed several planning priorities: first, a row of the glazed-blue bookcases should be placed against the wall beside the window, which is not only the background highlight

popular with lots of cyber celebrities and food bloggers, but also to create a cultural ambience for the store.

Second, having a long American-style table coupled with a row of lazy and comfortable sitting couches, variety of single chairs, end-view cabinets, pillows, and floor lamps matched eclectically to create a unique space that also meets the needs of the flow of customers to maintain a pleasant atmosphere to accompany the delicacies and pastries.

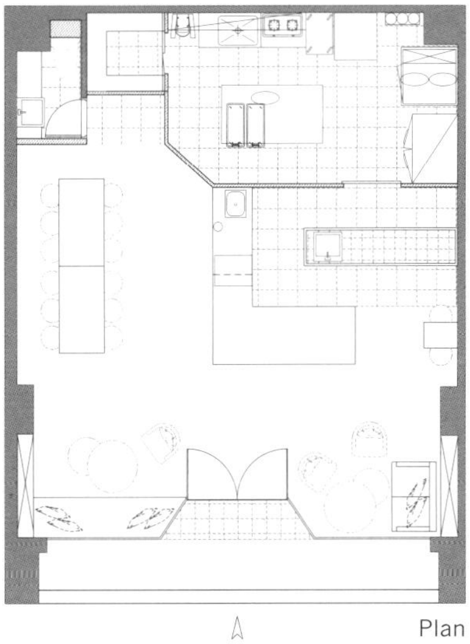

Plan

Oyster plus workshop

- **Project name**
  Pain Paulin Bakery
- **Location**
  Lège-Cap-Ferret, France
- **Site area**
  775 square feet
  (72 square meters)
- **Completion**
  2017
- **Interior design**
  Ciguë
- **Photography**
  Maris Mezulis

Pain Paulin bakery, a project designed by Ciguë in Cap Ferret, France, is the passionate story of a man who decided to drop everything to become a baker.

The client, Paulin, contacted the designers for the first time in 2012 to tell them that he wanted to work with them—and only them—in three years, when he would have quit his job and completed his bakery training. Every year, on the same date, he called to make sure the designers had not forgotten about him. At the end of 2015, as planned, he was ready and the project kicked off.

The designers found themselves juggling between the conservative setting of the Cap Ferret and the desire to build something elegant and contemporary.

Instead of seeing the local urban planning regulations as a constraint, Ciguë used them as a force to drive the project. Oyster shacks are pretty much what defines the area; it is the local reference, both mentally and

physically, the shack is the Cap. The client, however, had a modern bakery in mind, offering transparency on the entire baking process, from the flour sacks to the baking.

The designers decided to go for a collage of 'shack+lab': a shack on the top floor, dedicated to the accommodation and entirely made from wood, black on the outside, natural on the inside; and a lab underneath for the bakery, mainly glass, steel, and concrete.

The shack is intimate and warm; it's the living space, the home. The burnt Douglas wood cladding gives a feeling of protection and privacy, whilst the terraces and mezzanines offer bay views and create streams of indirect sunlight.

The lab, on the other hand, is bright and opens up onto the street and the city, welcoming all wandering eyes. The lack of building surface forged the modularity of the work and sales counter that gives its particularity to the bakery. It's an open working space, where traditions and expertise are shared. It's covered in white tiles upon which a collection of wheeled machines and tools can be moved around and rearranged according to different tasks or times of the day.

LA DOBLÉ 3.00
LA DOBLÉ GRAINÉE 3.60
LA BAGUETTOR 2.50
LE CORPS VIVANT 2.60
LE SINGLE MAN 2.90
LA TOURTE 18.80
LA BORDELAISE 7.60
LE CAMPAGNE 5.80
LE MOULÉ NATURE 2.60
LE GRAINÉ 6.90
LE MOULÉ GRAINÉ 3.10
L' OLIVE 5.00
LE NOIX 24.00
LE COMPLET 12.00
LE BI 6.90
LE PAIN DE L'EST 4.50
LA GRANDE BELLEZZA 3.90
LE PETIT ÉPEAUTRE 24.00
LE KHORASAN 5.90
LE LIBERTY NATURE 5.40
LE LIBERTY GRAINÉ 6.30

Section 1

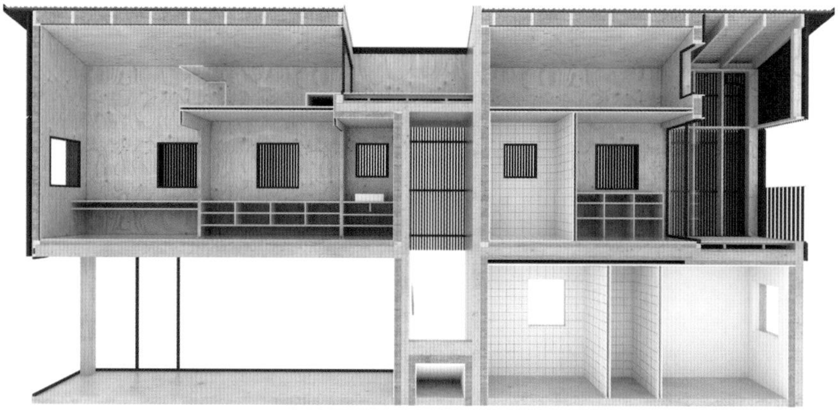

Section 2

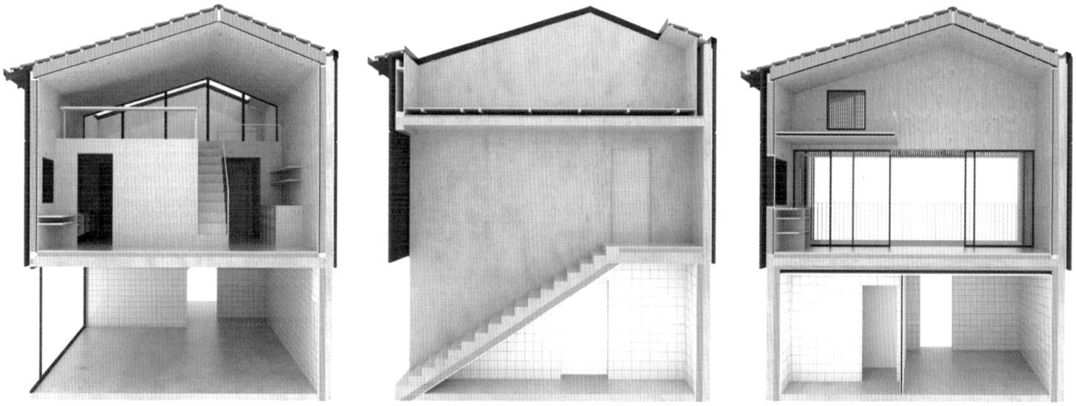

Simplified space design full of sense of ceremony

- **Project name**
  Tôt le Matin Boulangerie
- **Location**
  Nagoya, Japan
- **Site area**
  710 square feet
  (66 square meters)
- **Completion**
  2018
- **Interior design**
  Airhouse (Keiichi Kiriyama)
- **Photography**
  Toshiyuki Yano

The shop is located in a renovated building in the Meito district of Nagoya. Its name, Tôt le Matin, means "early in the morning" in French. The "M" from "Matin" inspired the motif for the lattice on the façade, but its shape also evokes ears of wheat, mountain ridges at dawn, and the slashes cut into French bread before baking. This slanted lattice thus serves as a symbol of the shop, expressing the desire to connect people with the business.

The client requested a space that was simple and chic but also evoked the spirituality of Japanese shrines and temples. Designers therefore aligned the entrance to the kitchen so that it symmetrically faces the sales counter, symbolically deifying and drawing attention to the kitchen to produce a kind of tension similar to what one feels when facing the gods at a shrine.

However, in order to simplify construction work and minimize the number of elements that had to be fabricated, designers limited new items to the wall separating the kitchen and sales area, the

table for displaying bread, and the exterior wall and front door. The other walls were simply stripped of their existing finishes to expose the concrete, while part of the existing ceiling was removed in the sales area, leaving the underlying lightweight steel framework in place to create a sense of height. Pendant lights and plants counteract the cool mood of the interior; when bread—which plays a central role in the design—is added, the space comes into balance.

By designing a unique shop that nevertheless did not require unnecessarily complex construction work, designers hope to have created a place where beginnings unfold, and where the owner will be able to achieve his goal of offering up delicious bread at the start of every day.

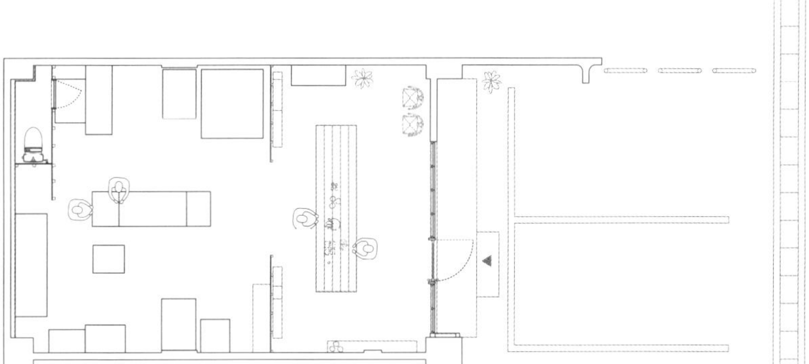

Plan

Fusion of modern and industrial styles

- **Project name**
  Tserki
- **Location**
  Paros island, Greek
- **Site area**
  1292 square feet
  (120 square meters)
- **Completion**
  2015
- **Interior design**
  STIRIXIS Group
- **Photography**
  Stavros Niflis

STIRIXIS Group, the internationally awarded strategy-through-execution consultancy firm, created an original pastry shop concept in Paros, one of the most famous Greek islands. It all started when a young couple contacted the STIRIXIS Group team to develop a distinctive pastry shop, one that would combine both modern and traditional elements. The name “Tserki” is the word for the metal cake ring used in pastry making, and it was chosen to highlight the freshness of the products, as the production also happens in the store’s kitchen.

Aiming at creating the best concept according to the client’s requests and the regional needs, the strategic goals and key project objectives were defined and taken into consideration in the design. The main design goal was to create a unique pastry shop that addressed the needs of a modern retail space. At the same time, the store had to match its surroundings, considering that it is part of a typical Cycladic-style property.

The 1292-square-foot (120-square-meter) space was fully utilized to create a

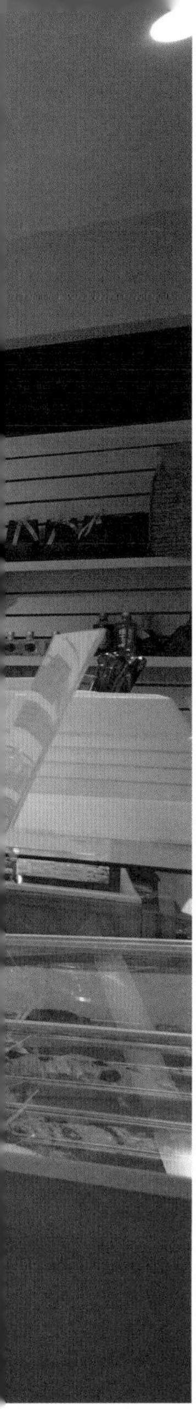

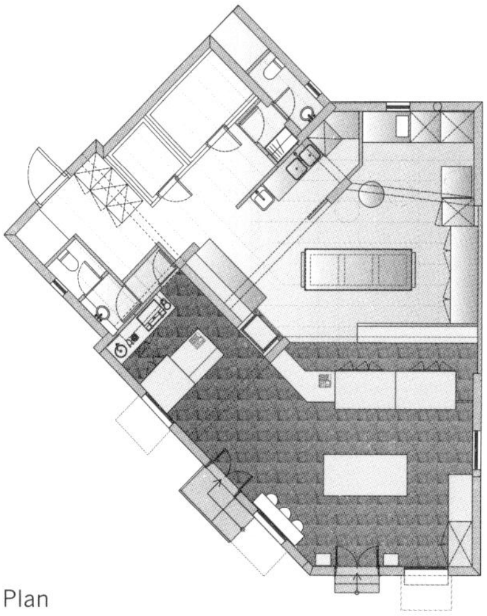

Plan

functional and impressive result. For balancing modern and traditional elements, a quite modern industrial look and feel was designed, using stylish fridges and windows and furniture with thin lines. The dominant colors used through the store were gray and black to balance the environment's image with the colorful products offered in the store. Additionally, the designers added some traditional details in shapes and finishing, such as ornamented floor tiles, lights, wooden shelves, and partitions to create an old-style but modern result.

High importance was also given to optimizing the customer flow and functionality. The placement of two doors on the two sides of the store make the visitors' movements within the space much easier and faster—this way, traffic issues during rush hours are avoided.

The logo is visible from far away but without disturbing the image of the environment. As such, Tserki was transformed into a delicious destination for a relaxing break and tasty snacks with a wide variety of both sweet and savory flavors for any time of the day and all occasions, including breakfast, lunch, coffee breaks, birthdays, and dinner with friends at home.

One of a kind Terrazo bar

- **Project name**
  Suzette
- **Location**
  Esplanade, Singapore
- **Site area**
  237 square feet
  (22 square meters)
- **Completion**
  2017
- **Interior design**
  The Strangely Good, OWMF Architecture
- **Photography**
  The Strangely Good, OWMF Architecture

This retro chic haven of a dessert bar is not only for those with a sweet tooth, it is eye candy for passers-by. Enter the Suzette and you will be greeted by the bar made up of customized terrazzo slabs with three colors in wavy swirl, which bore a time consuming yet fulfilling process of creating these one-of-a-kind terrazzo tiles, akin to the process of creating a cake with a cake mould and allowing it to "set." The reward is a truly unique showpiece of Suzette. Setting atop a floor with copper disc drops and chiseled cement, it is simply the icing of more extraordinary to come.

The clever detailing accorded to the form and function speaks for themselves, where dessert bar counter is served by cake keepers clamped onto counter. The details extend to the customized furniture. If having your cake on an odd-shaped marble table with hexagonal copper legs catches your fancy, Suzette is as irreverent as its offerings and sweet endings.

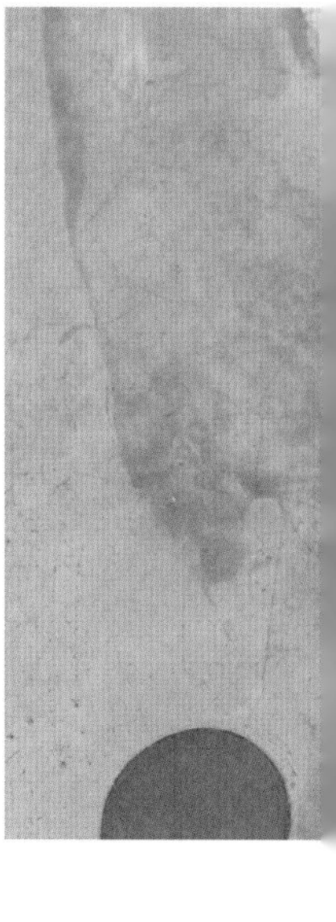

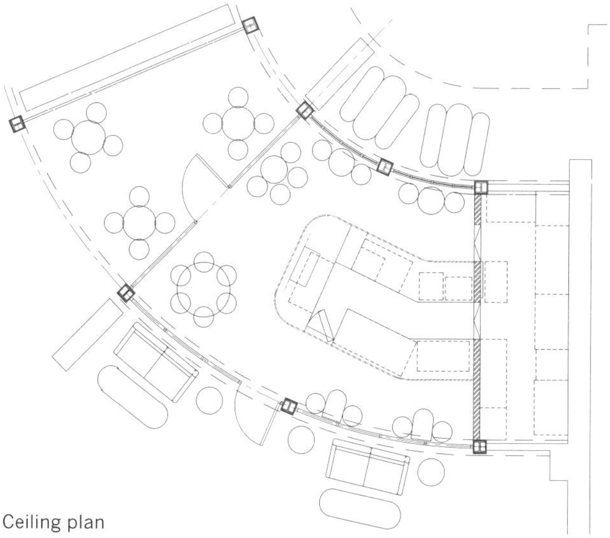

Ceiling plan

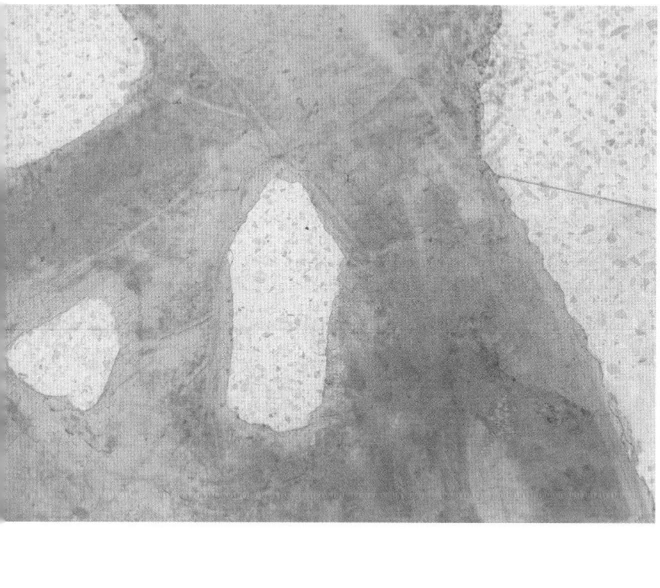

White space with brightness and delicacy

- **Project name**
  Commercial Axis Bakery
- **Location**
  Guimarães, Portugal
- **Site area**
  1033 square feet
  (96 square meters)
- **Completion**
  2017
- **Interior design**
  Martins Architecture Office
- **Photography**
  NUDO

A 32-year-old bakery needed a refurbishment to endorse a new contemporary image. The proposal was based on a commercial movement over the marble limit that contained in itself the products index. Through that line, the space was organized on a perpendicular axis (from the entrance pendulum), which meant to improve two moments of perception: generic display (on the bottom wall shelves) and a particular approach (three sets of products: bread, food, and cakes).

The employee point-in-space strategy is similar. Firstly, the fast consumption client and, secondly, the ones seated at the tables with other rhythms and types of consumption.

The construction process needed to be as fast and efficient as possible to reduce expenses and to allow the store to return to their routines. All the space was subject to infrastructure intervention ensuring that the production area was constructively as pragmatic as possible

while the commercial area was the most delicate one.

The production area was lined with washable and hygienically regulated materials; the commercial area explored the materiality, atmosphere, and scale of the space. There is a lacquered wooden base that absorbs the white paint differently from the plasterboard, thus this difference established a human scale aligned with the door heights. This human-scale line breaks its continuity in the existing windows proposing a geometric disruption.

The shelves on the wall needed a very strict steel sub-structure that would withstand the weight of the product samples (designing a kind of scenario) and that would also be lighted behind in order to mark that presence. Therefore, it was intended to differentiate two lighting layers for specific moments of space usage. The circled ring illuminated on its interior acts in this interest but most of all it adds a certain sense of gravity to the center of the space, which provides differentiated moments in space within an incredibly small area.

The gradually unfolding pure space

- **Project name**
  Les Bébés Cupcakery
- **Location**
  Taipei, Taiwan, China
- **Site area**
  1615 square feet
  (150 square meters)
- **Completion**
  2013
- **Interior design**
  J.C. Architecture
- **Photography**
  Kyle You

Upon the success of the first Les Bébés Cupcakery store using the simple concept of "folding"—as in the box package of cakes themselves—to create the best store space to display the cupcakes, the designer and owner wondered how to continue the spatial concept of folding and its brand spirit to fold out space in the second store.

The designer went back to the packaging box itself and recorded a string of "actions" of dismantling and assembling. However, he recorded the entire process of "packaging" rather than merely folding a space, echoing customers' experience in the store.

The designer took the box surface off and simplified it down to its structural frame. With four different folding steps—0-, 30-, 47-, and 90-degree angles—the designer folded the box from its original state to a three-dimensional object, and created a series of changing processes in these four angles. So the transition from the exterior façade to the interior façade and the

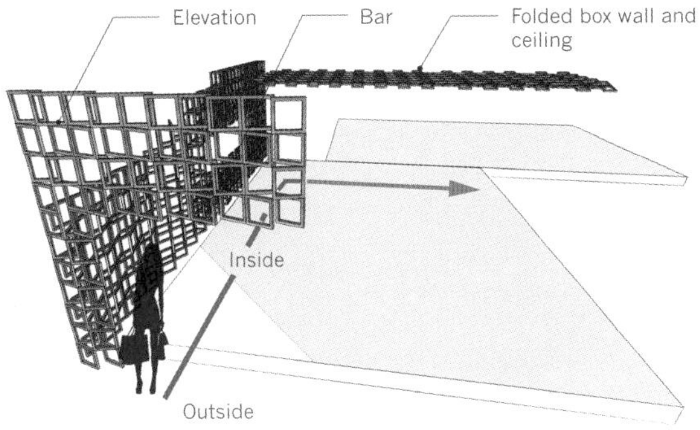

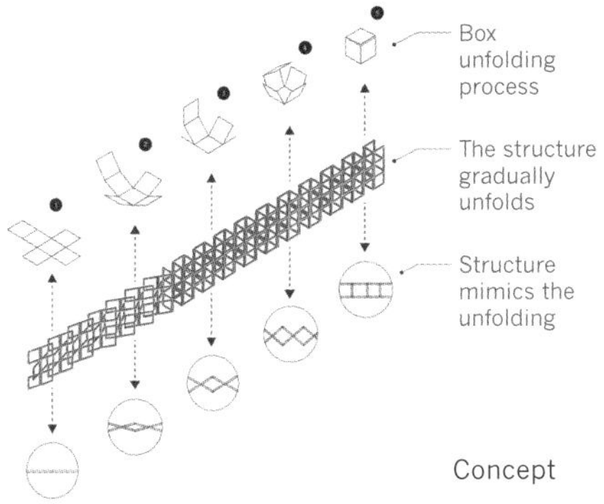

Concept

ceiling offers a wonderful journey of food discovery and excitement.

The project applied various building materials, such as white and black hard-wearing wooden flooring, a charcoal-grey ceiling, and white-painted walls. The table top of the counter was decorated in drana white marble.

Upon stepping into the store, the cupcakes are immediately in sight, and the delicate and lovely tray and display case provoke the appetite. For customers, this sense of delight, surprise, and freshness from the takeout area to the café area is the same as in the Qingtian store. With simple color matching and a delightful atmosphere, the cupcakes and baked goods are the main characters of the space. The architectural space, the cakes, and their packaging remerged into a successful bakery brand.

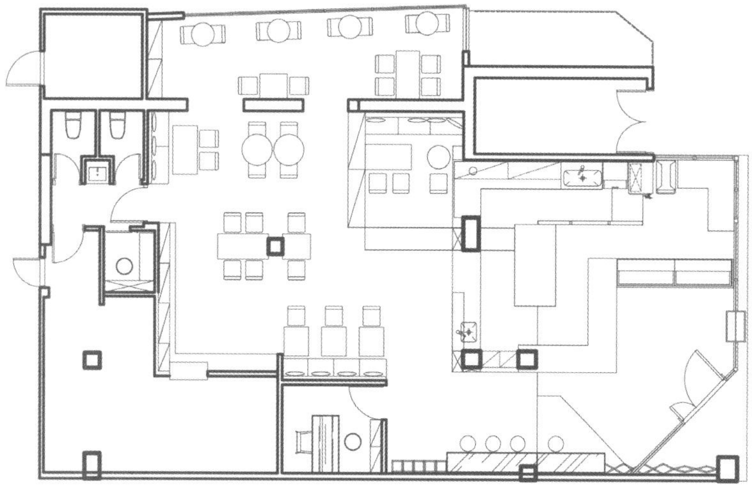

Plan

Dark space full of mystery

- **Project name**
  Sweet Alchemy
- **Location**
  Athens, Greece
- **Site area**
  1033 square feet
  (96 square meters)
- **Completion**
  2012
- **Interior design**
  Stelios Kois, Nikos Patsiaouras, Marielina Stavrou, Filippos Manolas
- **Photography**
  Giorgos Sfakianakis

The project was to design of the new Sweet Alchemy pastry shop in Athens, Greece. The store is located in the up-market suburb of Kifisia in the northern region of Athens. The client was Stelios Parliaros, who is considered to be the best patisserie in Greece and is also the author of many culinary books and host of a very popular patisserie show on Greek TV.

The word 'alchemy' arouses the notion of darkness, mystery, and mysticism practiced in laboratories full of peculiar enigmatic devices, rare distils, crystals, and potions. These images were the starting point for the development of a central idea, the recreation of this atmosphere in a contemporary outtake.

The space was characterized by the high degree of transparency, which was manipulated in order to diffuse the light and filter the optic penetration. The role of light was highly regarded and thoroughly studied since the beginning in order to create a unique solution for the particular

location and user. Light and shadow change throughout the day, giving the space a unique atmosphere every moment. Serenity is followed by tension and drama.

The punctured bronze skin of the main façades creates the impression of the chamber of treasures, of the golden cage, which encloses the precious, the rare commodity, the sin of the pleasure of the forbidden fruit.

The philosophy behind the choice of materials was in tune with the philosophy of the client. The selection of raw materials—iron, bronze, copper, and wood—were chosen for their natural characteristics and were only processed but not altered, in order to retain the natural appearance.

The designers' purpose was not the stenographic representation of a mystic environment but the formulation of the spirit of the place, the 'genius loci,' the atmosphere that will saturate the space and will transform it to a true place with its very own distinctive character. The sense of mythical, the mysterious discovery, and the transition to another reality were the characteristics of the Sweet Alchemy project of Stelios Parliaros and those that the designers wanted to transfuse into the new store.

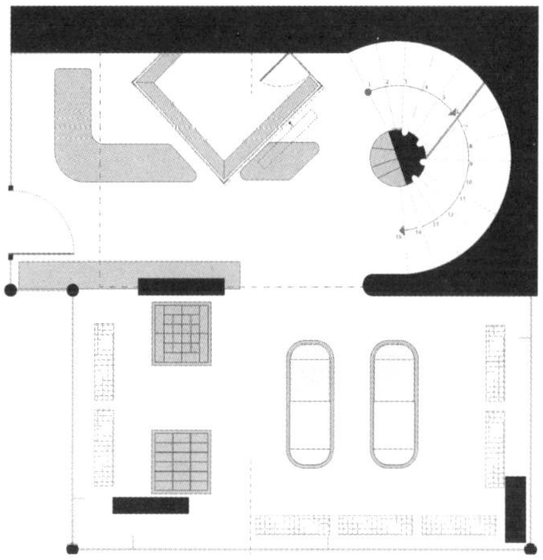

First-floor plan

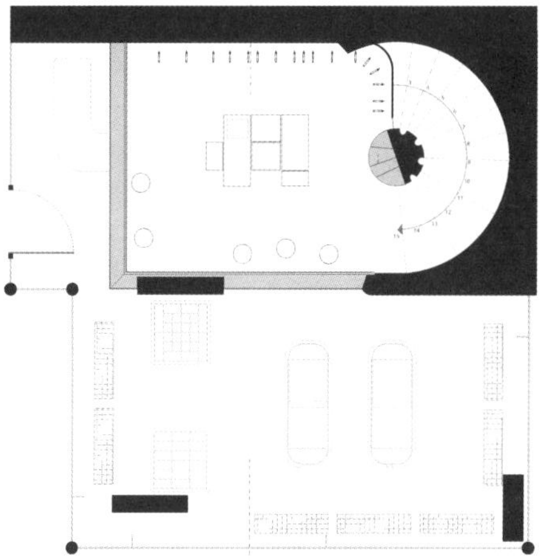

Mezzanine plan

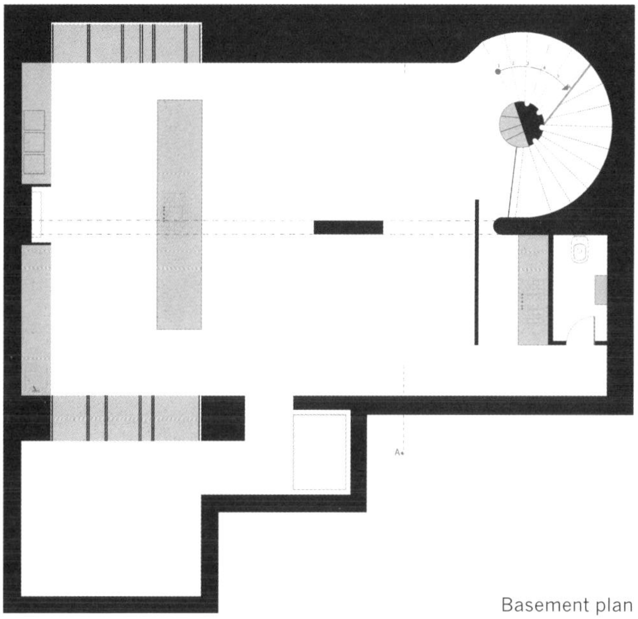

Basement plan

Index

Lukstudio
PP 114, 122
www.lukstudiodesign.com
press@lukstudiodesign.com

MAG arquiteturas
P 148
www.facebook.com/
magarquiteturas
b@bernardodemagalhaes.com.br

Manousos Leontarakis & Associates
P 180
www.manousosleontarakis.gr
info@manousosleontarakis.gr

Margstudio
PP 44, 94
www.margstudio.info
info@margstudio.com

Martins Architecture Office
P 228
www.m-ao.pt
i@m-ao.pt

mode:lina™
P 54
www.modelina-architekci.com
hello@modelina-architekci.com

naturehumaine
P 40
naturehumaine.com
media@naturehumaine.com

odd
P 196
www.odd-space.com
contact@odd-space.com

OWMF Architecture
P 224
owmf.net
owmf@owmf.net

PARAT
P 72
buero-parat.de
info@buero-parat.de

party/space/design
P 174
partyspacedesign.com
info@partyspacedesign.com

Paulo Merlini arquitectura
P 48
paulomerlini.com
press@paulomerlini.com

Rungta.co.,ltd
P 136
www.rungta.jp
haga@rungta.jp

SNARK
P 166
www.snark.cc
press@snark.cc

STIRIXIS Group
P 222
stirixis.com
advance@stirixis.com

Studio Etienne Bastormagi
P 200
etiennebas.com
info@etiennebas.com

Studio SKLIM
P 62
sklim.com
info@sklim.com

TAO (Trace Architecture Office)
P 160
www.t-a-o.cn
media@t-a-o.cn

Todor Cosmin Studio
P 152
www.todorcosmin.com
todorcosmin77@gmail.com

TZOKAS architects
P 24
www.tzokasarchitects.com
atzokas@yahoo.gr

Zemberek Design
PP 100, 104
www.zemberek.org
info@zemberek.org

Zones design Studio
P 206
zonesdesign.cn/zones
zones_design@yeah.net

Published in Australia in 2019 by
The Images Publishing Group Pty Ltd
Shanghai Office
ABN 89 059 734 431
6 Bastow Place, Mulgrave, Victoria 3170, Australia
Tel: +61 3 9561 5544 Fax: +61 3 9561 4860
books@imagespublishing.com
www.imagespublishing.com

The Images Publishing Group Reference Number: 1515

NATIONAL LIBRARY OF AUSTRALIA

A catalogue record for this book is available from the National Library of Australia

Title: Bakery Design
ISBN: 9781864708295

Printed by Everbest Printing Investment Limited, in Hong Kong/China